ASTROLOGY
FOR
MYSTICS

"I found *Astrology for Mystics* refreshing with its holistic approach to the water element. Tayannah Lee McQuillar is clearly a solid astrologer who adds her own perceptive insights to this book, including the significant fundamental equivalence of water signs, houses, and mysticism. As a person with long-term and personal interest in the subject, I can say that it substantially added to my astrological knowledge and personal understanding of the fourth, eighth, and twelfth houses."

FREDERICK HAMILTON BAKER,
AUTHOR OF *ALCHEMICAL TANTRIC ASTROLOGY*

"An intriguing and unusual book about the most mysterious of the elements. Mystics may not need to be astrologers, but astrologers do need to be mystics, so both have something to learn here."

ALISON CHESTER-LAMBERT, MA,
AUTHOR OF *GREEK MYTHOLOGY READING CARDS* AND
ASTROLOGY READING CARDS

"The fourth, eighth, and twelfth houses are the most mysterious and difficult to understand, and much of that is due to their connections to mysticism and the deep work of the soul. *Astrology for Mystics* openly and honestly explores these shadowy areas in the birth chart, casting light into the places just beyond those dark doors and making them more accessible to seekers who may have been too intimidated to enter. Tayannah Lee McQuillar gently leads the reader into the element of water flowing through our unconscious minds and hearts and invites us to explore its depths."

RAVEN KALDERA,
AUTHOR OF *PAGAN ASTROLOGY*

ASTROLOGY
FOR
MYSTICS

Exploring the Occult Depths
of the Water Houses in
Your Natal Chart

TAYANNAH LEE McQUILLAR

Destiny Books

Rochester, Vermont

Destiny Books
One Park Street
Rochester, Vermont 05767
www.DestinyBooks.com

Text stock is SFI certified

Destiny Books is a division of Inner Traditions International

Copyright © 2021 by Tayannah Lee McQuillar

Cataloging-in-Publication Data for this title is available from the Library of Congress

ISBN 978-1-64411-051-5 (print)
ISBN 978-1-64411-052-2 (ebook)

Printed and bound in the United States by Lake Book Manufacturing, Inc.
The text stock is SFI certified. The Sustainable Forestry Initiative® program promotes sustainable forest management.

10 9 8 7 6 5 4 3 2 1

Text design and layout by Virginia Scott Bowman
This book was typeset in Garamond Premier Pro, Frutiger, and Gill Sans with Majesty and Fnord used as display typefaces

To send correspondence to the author of this book, mail a first-class letter to the author c/o Inner Traditions • Bear & Company, One Park Street, Rochester, VT 05767, and we will forward the communication, or contact the author directly at **tlmcquillar@gmail.com**.

Contents

What Is a Mystic?

ACCORDING TO THE DICTIONARY, *mystic* is defined as "involving or having the nature of an individual's direct subjective communion with God or ultimate reality." The dictionary definition is not universal but is just one of several possible meanings of what a mystic is, as in other cultures the concept of objective or subjective experience may or may not even exist. What we do know for certain is that there have been people in every society who removed themselves (mentally and/or physically) from the popular religious or philosophical paradigm in order to connect with the divine on their own terms. That being the case, mystics have always inspired awe, fear, respect, or loathing among people who function comfortably within exoteric or mainstream boundaries. However, it is important for me to mention that just because people are mystics doesn't mean that they are automatically antagonistic toward conventional teachings. Mystics may discover, after years of contemplation that they are more in alignment with the spiritual beliefs they grew up with than they thought. The mystic is not interested in rebellion for its own sake or in proving or disproving anything to anyone else. All mystics desire is the freedom to seek, define, and interpret reality according to their own conscience without interference.

Mystics and Esoteric Astrology

Mystics are the foundation of all religious and spiritual systems in the world. Someone, somewhere, at some time had to be the first to wonder if what she was being told about the divine was true and to seek a direct mystical experience in order to confirm or deny it for herself. Then, from that experience, that person formed ideas regarding the truth or nature of existence. Those ideas formed a narrative, then a counternarrative by default, and, finally, rites and rituals that utilize symbolism from the mystic's narrative to celebrate and recreate the sacred for everyone else. Most people perceive the mystic as a peripheral character in discussions pertaining to religion when the truth is that the mystic is always at the center.

It is in the nature of a mystic to explore that which is unapparent, so it should be no surprise that mystics have contemplated the esoteric meaning of the zodiac. Unlike today, astrology was considered a practical subject for people to study before medicine, agriculture, fashion, etc., were divorced from the stars in the consciousness of the average person. Post the Age of Enlightenment, if a person studied astrology, the mere interest in the subject itself made that person "mystical" to many. So if a mystic lived prior to the eighteenth century, then the occult would not be astrology itself but the hidden significance of the signs, planets, houses, and so forth beyond that which had been consistently written and agreed upon by consensus for centuries. The insights of mystics regarding the true nature of the zodiac, astrology's ultimate purpose, or how the data from one's birth chart should be perceived or utilized by individuals may or may not be agreed upon by traditional astrologers. In fact, they may find interpretations outside of the accepted canon or any attempts to mystify what they consider to be simply mathematics absolutely ridiculous, and that's fine. *Astrology for Mystics* is the book you chose because you wanted to consider or contemplate something new; therefore, how other people, including the experts, feel about whatever you get out of this experience is irrelevant.

At the core of mysticism is the ability to interpret symbols—to observe one's external and internal landscape with honest eyes. We, as personalities, as our experiences, are merely a conglomeration of symbol via the narrative of our lives. Therefore, it makes no difference whether one is contemplating a teacup or a constellation—your interpretation of its ultimate purpose, of its usefulness, of its beauty, or of its flaws will be informed by a collage of images that is your memory. These images, when distilled for the essential truths they reveal, may then be trusted to accurately guide the consciousness to clarify what one sees in the sky.

That, coupled with the observation of repetitive astronomical patterns and the effects certain constellations have on crops, animals, and other aspects of nature, then births a new biography of the galaxy. Of course, this would only be possible if the viewer had released the fear of being wrong; otherwise, the imagination would be restricted to revolving around that which has already been established or promoted as fact by the aristocracy or another privileged class, who are regarded as the judges of what is true and what is false, what is sane and what is insane. It is useful to align the norms of the ruling class to everything above the head or below the feet of their subjects in order to sacralize societal systems, thus, significantly reducing the possibility of rebellion, as to rebel against custom would then become an offense to the cosmos, the stars, and everything connected to or associated with them, including flora and fauna or maybe even one's ancestors. Humans have always linked their ways to the ways of the gods, however that concept is realized or understood.

In my own practice, I consider the imagery and explanations

inherited from the ancients, but I also consider what each sign or planet signifies according to my own life experience. For example, I try to observe and note patterns of what happens to me on days when the moon is in a particular sign. After about two years I may notice that my skin tends to break out more often when the moon is in Leo. I may also recognize that my grandfather tends to call, my hair gets dry, or other things regularly occur during specific lunar positions.

The same can be said for other phenomena like retrogrades and eclipses. I consider the forecasts of experts regarding what may happen and then I integrate it or reject it based on my own experience. I allow my intuition to tell me what does or does not apply, and I permit myself to be the final authority.

I am not an astrologer. I am merely one who contemplates the wisdom that has been passed down by astrologers throughout the ages for the purpose of self-knowledge. This, if done long enough, inevitably leads to the appreciation of the beauty and complexity of other people, the elements, and the innumerable symbols that humans utilize in the attempt to comprehend and explain modalities and realities.

Do I consider myself a mystic? Absolutely. It is acknowledged by many that there is much to learn by what is said; however, the wise know that there is much more to contemplate and realize based on what is not. That basic truth may be applied to astrology or any other subject. There are profound truths in between the lines, and I enjoy contemplating what those might be.

In other words, this book uses common astrological knowledge as a scaffold in the process of creating an individualized occult philosophy and spiritual regimen, one that doesn't require you to believe anyone else, follow everyone else, or become someone else. I thought it would be useful to have information about the possibilities contained within the water houses in one book for the convenience of occultists who may be seeking more ways to personalize their spiritual practice. The purpose of this book is to assist you in the realization of your own potential, talents, and abilities that traditionally fall under the domain of the fourth, eighth, and twelfth houses.

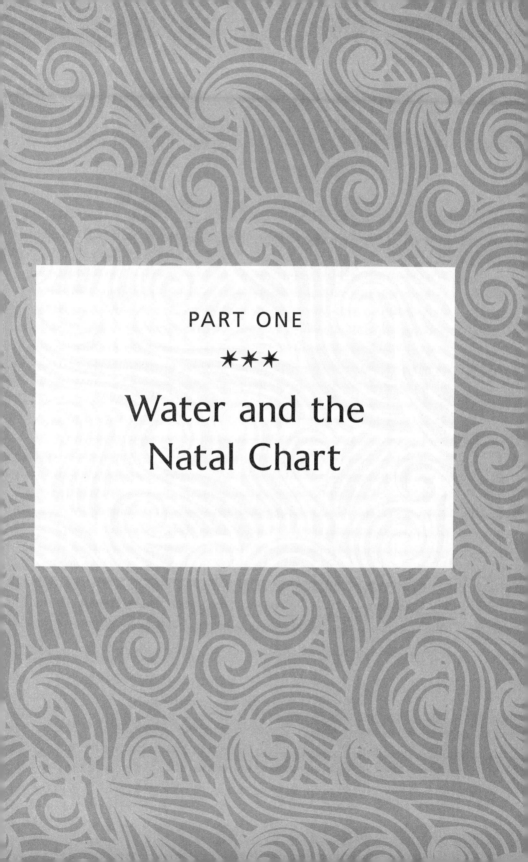

PART ONE

★★★

Water and the Natal Chart

Exploring the Occult Depths

The Esoteric Significance of Water

WE ALL KNOW THAT WATER COVERS the majority of the Earth's surface, that our bodies are made of approximately 60 percent water, and that we cannot live without it. But what, exactly, is water? Well, we know that chemically water is an odorless, colorless substance made of billions of molecules. Each molecule of water consists of three atoms: two hydrogen atoms with one oxygen atom, written as H_2O. Water is found in three different states—liquid, solid, and gas. The temperature determines which form water takes. As liquid, water flows as streams, rivers, and oceans; as a solid it is in the form of ice, and as a gas it is vapor in the atmosphere. We learned about the form and function of water in primary school, but this explanation doesn't exactly tell us what water actually is at a deeper level. The reason for this is simple: it is because no one knows.

The Esoteric Meaning of Water

Water is believed to be the first element from which all things, both terrestrial and divine, ultimately originated. Every culture around the world has an abundance of myths and folklore that center around water because our reliance on this primary substance is universal. Almost all creation stories since time immemorial include the mention of primeval waters as the precursor of life. So it's not a surprise that water is associated with depth, magic, mystery, darkness, emotions, truth, consciousness, spirituality, birth, and rebirth. Water is also associated with time and wisdom because of its cyclical nature. There is no new water. The water that was here in the beginning is the same water our ancestors drank and is the same water we are drinking now. Everything alive, no matter how it looks and where it dwells on our planet, is nourished, sustained, and informed by the exact same source.

Water has several unique and awesome qualities that align with occult and esoteric teachings even more so than the other elements of air, earth, and fire. Water is so flexible that it may transform into any shape depending on the vessel in which it is held. This is easily analogized to the knowledge that we all come from the same source and only our vessels (our minds and souls) make us different. We may not be able to change that which is fundamental to the survival of human life, but we can certainly change our beliefs. This, in turn, when enough people move on from a particular narrative, changes the world.

Everything was born from watery substance so it only made sense that one could be cleansed or reborn from water. Thus, spiritual baths and ritual cleansing are ubiquitous. Water can facilitate healing on its own and join forces with other elements to increase its potency. We bathe in mineral springs and the oceans to rejuvenate, and soak herbs, stones, and many other objects in our water before we drink it. Unlike the other elements, the power in water has the capability of becoming a part of us when we consume it. That's not practical, pleasant, or as easy to do with the other elements.

Water washes away dirt in the form of substances, grime, and people. There are many flood stories from various cultures around the world that state that the creator flushes away evildoers when he's had enough.

The Spiritual History of Water

It is my theory that water, like all of the other elements, has been considered sacred as long as humans have existed. We realized that water gushed from our mothers before life appeared and that water is an absolute requirement for sustaining life. This substance, therefore, must be divine, as it is essential to existence itself.

Flood Myths

According to the Lenape Indians, there was a great flood that was so devastating that only a few humans were able to survive it by riding on the back of an old turtle shell. A muskrat managed to save all life on Earth by placing land on the turtle shell from which the whole world grew. Afterward, people were able to repopulate the planet.

In one of the spiritual myths of Hawaii related to floods, there was a sea-dwelling woman named Lalohona. She was seduced into coming ashore, to the great displeasure of her parents, who subsequently sent a deluge. The objective was to find their lost daughter by utilizing the assistance of fish, and everything went back to normal after she was found.

In Papua New Guinea, it was believed that a great flood covered the Earth except for the peak of Mount Tauga. When all seemed to be lost, all life on Earth was suddenly saved by the sacred serpent they call Radaulo, who managed to intimidate the sea into retreat with his fiery tongue.

There is a ubiquitous message of the redemptive power of the water element after moral transgression or defilement that can be found all around the world. It is implied that this in and of itself is "magic."

The Role of Water in Hoodoo

In hoodoo, water is used to cleanse, curse, heal, and charge objects and people. The source (lake, stream, river, ocean) and the local lore associated with a particular body of water are given great consideration, as selecting an inappropriate one could neutralize the work or even bring misfortune. "Water" from the body in the form of menstrual blood, tears, and urine is also frequently utilized to personalize a working, often for the purpose of domination or protection.

Water Spirits

Water spirits, goddesses, and gods abound in many traditions. Below are just a few that illustrate the spiritual significance of water.

Atabey is the self-created mother goddess of the indigenous people of the Caribbean islands, namely Boriken (Puerto Rico) and Quisqueya (Haiti and Dominican Republic). She was the spirit of the Earth itself and was worshipped as the goddess of all bodies of water. In addition to her nurturing aspect, she also had a "maiden" aspect called Caguana and a darker warrior aspect known as Guabancex who controlled storms, volcanoes, hurricanes, and earthquakes. She is the mother of the male aspect of the sea and fertility.

Ailsie is the Aniyunwiya (Cherokee) goddess of water and pools. All water that exists is the result of her tears after her father forbid her from marrying the one she loved. The name Ailsie means "devoted to God."

Ahone is the genderless creator god of the Powhatan people. It was generally referred to as a "great spirit." Ahone was considered such an auspicious force by nature that it required no offerings or sacrifices whatsoever. Ahone created water and was symbolized by the hare.

Mama Qucha is the ancient Incan goddess of fish and the sea, as well as all other bodies of water. Also called Cochamama, she was considered the protector of fisherman and sailors. As a primordial deity, Cochamama transcends our notions of time and space. She is older than the Earth and moon, who are her children.

Long before the arrival of any foreigners in Australia, aboriginal people had the concept of the mermaid. Yawkyawks ("young woman spirit beings"), as they are called, live in rock pools, freshwater springs, and waterholes. Their bodies are half fish and half human, their hair has the appearance of algae, and they have the unsurpassed ability to make women fertile. Yawkyawks are mostly nocturnal.

Susanoo no Mikoto is the Shinto god of the sea and storms. He is considered powerful, boisterous, and chaotic. However, his nature can be both malevolent and benevolent depending on the situation. According to Japanese mythology, a purification ritual known as harae is performed to reestablish balance and to prevent misfortune. Susanoo is also the father of the god of magic.

These are just six examples of water deities through which the water element is described as creative, destructive, transformative, protective, infinite, and older than human perceptions of it. These water spirits are also able to be negotiated with if their power is acknowledged and if we know exactly what to sacrifice in order to attain whatever we are seeking. This is also true of the water houses and how we relate to them. It reiterates what I said in the beginning, that the wisdom which may be attained by contemplating our relationship to this element via astrology is limitless.

The Earth Is an Evil and Watery Place

Contemporary people do not differ in any significant way from the ancients regarding their belief that living near water is relaxing and therapeutic, that water contains healing properties and may confer spiritual protection, transmit messages from the plant or mineral kingdom, and purify sin, and that it is a symbol of renewal. Millions of people of diverse ethnic, cultural, and religious backgrounds spend countless dollars dreaming of vacationing or living near bodies of water to rejuvenate; they prepare spiritual baths, cleanse and revitalize their faith using holy water, and commune with aquatic spirits and deities.

However, the difference between yesterday and today is the worldwide acceptance and tolerance of water pollution on a level the world has never seen before. One must then ask how humanity, who is so dependent on and utilizes this element arguably more than any other to commune with the sacred, has allowed the elite to normalize the sullying of our precious water supply? It may be because most people have access to inexpensive filtered and spring water. However, that only addresses how we have allowed ourselves to be pacified and how a substance essential to life on Earth has been monetized. It is my belief that people have forgotten how deeply ingrained narratives that originated in the distant past continue to affect their lives today. The reality is that the "civilized" Western world has had a love/hate relationship with water since the very beginning of the rise of Christianity.

The tolerance for polluted water may have begun with the acceptance of the doctrine of original sin. After Adam and Eve's fall from grace, the world ceased to be a paradise but became a wicked place filled with wicked people who were born flawed and in need of redemption. The newly empowered early church fathers couldn't wait to make a clear distinction between pagans and Christians. They decided that most things that humans found pleasurable were probably a sin that shouldn't be indulged in. While sex usually comes to mind, many people don't know that bathing was considered just as bad. The reason was that the Romans were considered immoral, as were other lascivious heathens who enjoyed washing their bodies and languishing in water. So not only did water encourage people to remain nude for an extended period of time (which implied sex) but it made people vain and prideful. Saint Benedict, patron saint of Europe, urged that for "those who are well, and especially the young, bathing shall seldom be permitted." As a result, Europeans only bathed a few times a year, if that, because being unwashed was considered a sign of holiness. This attitude only began to change after the cholera epidemic decimated the British population. So between the first century and the nineteenth century BCE, Europeans didn't care what they did to their water because they weren't washing and definitely didn't associate water with holiness outside of a few rites and rituals.

When Christianity and European world views spread around the globe as a result of conquer, commerce, and colonization, the dissociation and indifference to polluting water traveled with them.

In the innumerable instances when indigenous people rebelled against this offensive behavior, all resistance was discredited as typical of backward, inferior people and often crushed without mercy. Despite centuries of persecution, indigenous communities around the world continue to revolt against colonial governments and the mentality that allows the desecration of water to be perpetuated. In the meantime, cultures and communities that consider water the sacred dwelling place of their extended family in the form of aquatic animals, ancestors, gods, and goddesses are forced to endure the continual disrespect and the defilement of their rites and rituals because the dominant culture doesn't perceive the significance of water in the same way.

2

Practicing Mystical Astrology

*Incorporating the Water Houses
into Your Spiritual Life*

THE INFORMATION IN THIS BOOK is meant to be a starting point in your journey of self-discovery. My intention is for you to learn what has been said about the significance of the water signs and houses and then eventually use this information to explore and discover the consequence of these symbols in your own life. This book is meant to be a useful tool in constructing a spiritual regimen for yourself that is solely based on your individual strengths and weaknesses, utilizing the knowledge within the water houses as a guide. Obviously, I couldn't put everything there is to know on the subject in this one book, but I believe it is a great starting point for understanding your temperament as it pertains to spiritual matters and what you need to focus on most.

In addition to creating new practices, what you learn here could certainly be incorporated into any of the rites, rituals, and practices that you're doing now. It is intended to help strengthen your spiritual path and may help you to zero in on what aspects of the religious or spiritual teachings you currently follow that *you* need to focus on. For example, based on your fourth house sign placement and planets, maybe you as an individual don't need to meditate on that scripture or lesson that teaches one to be nurturing and charitable, because your mind and soul are already comfortable being and doing that. Or, if Cancer is in your fourth house, you might want to do ritual work related to the subjects ruled by Cancer in order to align the energy with your intention.

Instead of beating a dead horse, becoming inexplicably bored, or wondering why you don't connect with a particular system, now you may conclude that it's not about that at all. Perhaps many people are dissatisfied or don't feel they're growing into the most powerful version of themselves simply because they need a more personalized "workout" plan. There is simply no way you can grow and expand if you keep running to the same occult practices, sutras, inspirational quotes, etc., that you're comfortable with. Challenge yourself by going through each of the sign and planet chapters in this book and writing down at least three habits or patterns of thought that are holding you back the most, based on the placement of your houses and planets. Then flip to new verses in your holy text that address your shortcomings rather than stroke your ego or make you feel warm and fuzzy, sign up for an axe-throwing class instead of yoga, or become a volunteer at a soup kitchen because, well, you're kind of selfish. This is the best way to prevent yourself from becoming a "McSpiritualist" who is not interested in doing any work that involves leaving your comfort zone.

That said, it's important to be conscious of when you try to use your natal chart as an excuse for being a jerk, because that's not what this is about. Astrology is only a map and should not be considered a fortune telling device. *You* decide how much you will get out of life, depending on whether you are willing to put in the extra work. I mean this only in relation to spiritual growth. Not everyone is going to be rich, find their twin-flame connection, or be considered physically gorgeous, but everyone can choose to become better versions of themselves if that's what they desire. Otherwise, it's not about being "spiritual" at all but is merely a mockery of all the people named and unnamed who have helped put these systems into place for our benefit.

About the Water Signs

The element of water is associated with the signs Cancer, Scorpio, and Pisces, which rule the fourth, eighth, and twelfth houses, respectively. Any planet that inhabits a house will affect how that house functions as each planet has its own temperament. For example, if the Sun is in the eighth house, then it will "brighten" that house and serve to mitigate or modify any gloomy or difficult lessons that may have otherwise been very dark or heavy.

People born under water signs are sensitive, intuitive, emotional, family oriented, receptive, empathetic, artistic, psychic, compassionate, imaginative, creative, and nurturing and tend to be more introverted. Water is a very poor medium for sound, and so water signs are not informed by facts or external stimuli but primarily by their perceptions of things.

Water signs feel intensely, which may make them prone to romanticism, delusions, brooding, escapism, impracticality, moodiness, self-indulgence, and clinginess. They value deep, emotional connections with others, but it's important for them to make sure that desire doesn't lead to an unhealthy obsession. Water takes the shape of anything that possesses it. Likewise, water signs have to be especially mindful of the company they keep, for they can be extremely impressionable.

It's also wise for water signs to be careful not to hurt themselves in the process of helping others by being taking notice of when they're spreading themselves too thin.

Water signs appreciate beauty and sharing beauty with others, so they do best when they have an outlet to express their abundant creativity. They are also dreamers, so it is very important that they do not forget the importance of taking practical action and learning to apply what they know to improve their mundane, daily lives. Water signs have very vivid imaginations, so it's in their best interest to reflect seriously on the consequences of any flights of fancy. Water requires a vessel to contain it or it will flow all over the place and evaporate.

Water signs often have vivid dreams and should be encouraged to write these dreams down, because they usually contain important messages.

You will benefit from analyzing the pros and cons of the sign ruling each house sign as well as the sign occupying that house on your chart and compare it to how your personality aligns with those characteristics in an auspicious or disruptive way.

Signs and Houses of the Zodiac

Important Information from
Your Natal Chart

THE ZODIAC IS DIVIDED INTO TWELVE HOUSES that are each ruled by a different sign. The zodiac begins with the first house, which is ruled by the sign of Aries, and goes around counterclockwise until the twelfth house, ruled by Pisces. Each house is associated with different aspects of life, keynotes, traits, and events. The ruling sign of each house, which is predetermined and does not change, dictates what that house is about.

When a person is born, the planets are all in specific signs and houses, adding a more complex layer to how astrological influences may come to bear in your life. Astrologers interpret this information to determine individuals' possible past, present, and future life experiences as well as their potential obstacles and gifts. This will be different for each person depending on her or his birth chart. To understand the difference between the fixed ruling signs of the houses and the variable locations of astrological aspects in an individual's birth chart, you can think of the following: When guests visit your home they can change the atmosphere or vibe in your home but their presence doesn't change the architecture or décor. The activities and discussions will

certainly change depending on your guests' temperaments/interests/
relationships to you but, again, the home remains the same.

Determining Your Houses and Planets

There are plenty of websites that will generate a free astrology chart for
you, but I personally find Astrodienst (astro.com) to be the simplest
and easiest one to navigate.* Once you generate your chart, you will
see glyphs that represent the signs and planets; see the table on page 22
for a quick reference of what each glyph represents. The first thing you
must do is determine your rising sign, or ascendant, often abbreviated
ASC or AC, which is in your first house. Once you have determined
this you will be able to find which signs and planets are in your fourth,
eighth, and twelfth houses by moving in a counterclockwise direction.
Note that sometimes multiple planets fall in a single house and other
times houses contain no planets at all.

If you have a sign on the cusp, meaning it is within 29.2 degrees
of the next sign, then it is advisable just to focus on the meaning of
the actual sign that is in that house. For example, my moon sign is
1 degree Cancer; because of that, some people would read both Gemini
and Cancer moon forecasts, but I have determined that it would be
best for me to focus on Cancer. While I have no problem with the
preferences of others, as the author of this book, I recommend using
the meaning of the sign within each house as your guide.

For an example of how to read your chart for the purposes of
this book, take a look at groundbreaking actress and singer Dorothy

---

*Choose "Free Horoscopes" and click on "Chart drawing, Ascendant." You will be
asked to provide your name and birth data, and then you will be able to view your
birth chart showing in which signs your houses fall as well as where the planets fall
within the houses.

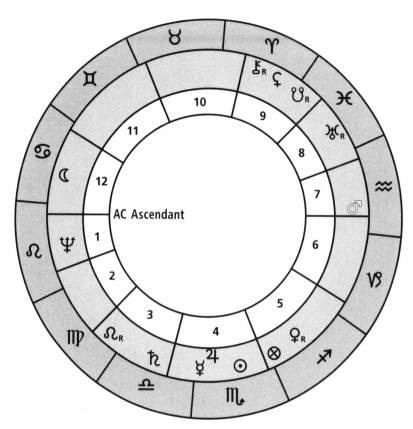

Dorothy Dandridge
November 9, 1922 at 10:35 pm
Cleveland, Ohio, United States

Dandridge's chart above. Dandridge was an actress during Hollywood's golden age and made history as the first Black actress to be nominated for the Academy Award for Best Actress for her role in *Carmen Jones*. Looking at her chart, you can see that her ascendant, or rising sign, is Leo, placing Leo in the first house in her birth chart. From there you can move three segments counterclockwise to find Virgo in her fourth house. Continuing counterclockwise you will find Pisces in her eighth house and Cancer in her twelfth house.

Signs		Planets	
♈	Aries	☉	Sun
♉	Taurus	☽	Moon
♊	Gemini	☿	Mercury
♋	Cancer	♀	Venus
♌	Leo	♂	Mars
♍	Virgo	♃	Jupiter
♎	Libra	♄	Saturn
♏	Scorpio	♅	Uranus
♐	Sagittarius	♆	Neptune
♑	Capricorn	♇	Pluto
♒	Aquarius	☊	North Node
♓	Pisces	⚷	Chiron

Basic Information about the Signs

Each zodiac sign has certain keywords, minerals, numbers, animals, and more associated with it. You can use these totems to create altar spaces or use them to guide your decisions when purchasing ritual clothing and spiritual supplies. For example, I have Libra in my eighth house, so I may choose to do deep eighth house meditations on a Friday while wearing an opal and burning pink candles. The sky is the limit in terms of how this information may be integrated into your own spiritual practice. The purpose of this book, however, is to encourage you to go beyond what has been suggested by others and make your own totems and correlations based on what your spirit tells you to do.

♈ Aries

Motto: I AM

Element: Fire

Lucky day: Tuesday

Lucky color: Bright red

Birthstone: Ruby

Lucky numbers: 7, 17, and 21

Best business partners: Scorpio, Libra, and Taurus

Best love matches: Leo and Sagittarius

♉ Taurus

Motto: I HAVE

Element: Earth

Lucky day: Friday

Lucky color: Leaf green

Birthstone: Emerald

Lucky numbers: 4, 6, 11

Best business partners: Gemini, Libra, Scorpio, and Sagittarius

Best love matches: Virgo and Capricorn

♊ Gemini

Motto: I THINK

Element: Air

Lucky day: Wednesday

Lucky colors: Lemon green and bright orange

Birthstone: Aquamarine

Lucky numbers: 3, 12, and 18

Best business partners: Cancer, Scorpio, Sagittarius, and Capricorn

Best love matches: Libra and Pisces

♋ Cancer

Motto: I FEEL

Element: Water

Lucky day: Monday

Lucky colors: White, silver, and light blue

Birthstones: Pearls and silver jewelry

Lucky numbers: 2, 8, and 12

Best business partners: Leo, Taurus, Capricorn, and Aquarius

Best love matches: Scorpio and Taurus

♌ Leo

Motto: I CAN

Element: Fire

Lucky day: Sunday

Lucky colors: Bright orange and gold

Birthstones: Ruby, sapphire, and gold jewelry

Lucky numbers: 1, 9, and 10

Best business partners: Virgo, Capricorn, Aquarius, and Taurus

Best love matches: Aries and Sagittarius

♍ Virgo

Motto: I ANALYZE

Element: Air

Lucky day: Wednesday

Lucky colors: Moss green, gray, brown

Birthstone: Emerald

Lucky numbers: 10, 15, and 27

Best business partners: Libra, Gemini, Pisces, and Taurus

Best love matches: Pisces and Cancer

♎ Libra

Motto: I WEIGH

Element: Air

Lucky day: Friday

Lucky colors: Pink and violet

Birthstones: Quartz and opal

Lucky numbers: 2, 8, and 19

Best business partners: Pisces, Taurus, and Gemini

Best love matches: Aquarius and Leo

♏ Scorpio

Motto: I DESIRE

Element: Water

Lucky day: Sunday

Lucky color: Crimson

Birthstones: Onyx, ruby, and topaz

Lucky numbers: 4, 13, and 21

Best business partners: Sagittarius, Aries, Taurus, and Gemini

Best love matches: Pisces and Cancer

♐ Sagittarius

Motto: I SEE

Element: Fire

Lucky day: Thursday

Lucky colors: Violet and purple

Birthstone: Turquoise

Lucky numbers: 9, 14, and 23

Best business partners: Capricorn, Taurus, Cancer, and Gemini

Best love matches: Leo, Aries, and Libra

♑ Capricorn

Motto: I ACHIEVE

Element: Earth

Lucky day: Saturday

Lucky colors: Black, gray, green, and brown

Birthstones: Onyx and topaz

Lucky numbers: 3, 16, and 25

Best business partners: Cancer, Scorpio, Libra, Virgo, and Leo

Best love matches: Cancer and Scorpio

♒ Aquarius

Motto: I KNOW

Element: Air

Lucky day: Wednesday

Lucky colors: Light blue and violet

Birthstone: Amethyst

Lucky numbers: 7, 14, and 20

Best business partners: Pisces, Cancer, Leo, and Scorpio

Best love matches: Leo, Libra, and Pisces

♓ Pisces

Motto: I BELIEVE

Element: Water

Lucky day: Monday

Lucky colors: Navy blue, sea green, and indigo

Birthstone: Topaz

Lucky numbers: 5, 11, and 19

Best business partners: Aries, Libra, and Virgo

Best love matches: Leo, Aries, and Taurus

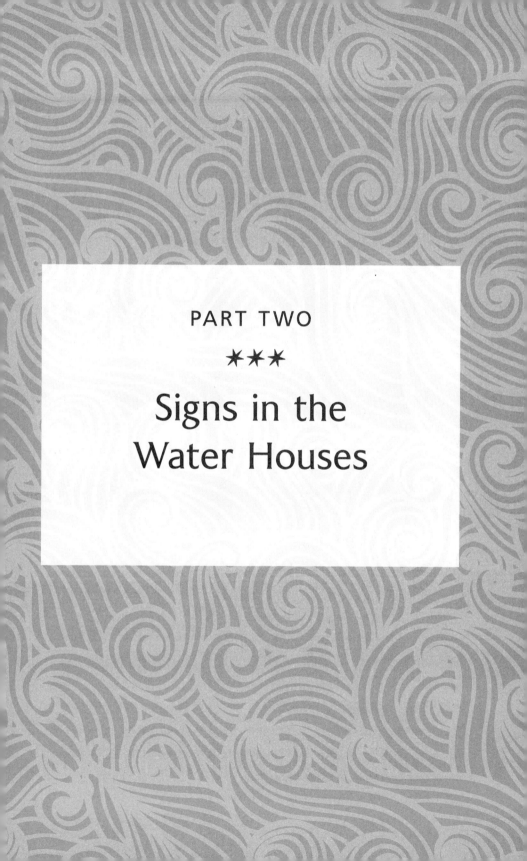

PART TWO

✦✦✦

Signs in the
Water Houses

The Significance of the Water Houses

THERE IS MUCH THAT CAN BE SAID ABOUT the qualities of all of the signs and houses, but the focus of this book is on the houses represented by the three water signs: Cancer, Scorpio, and Pisces. The water triad represents our emotional landscape, the lessons we need to learn in order to grow spiritually, and our potential occult talents, in addition to other more mundane aspects of life.

The Fourth House

The fourth house relates to Cancer, the fourth sign of the zodiac. The natural ruler of the fourth house is the moon. The fourth house is the house of home and family, of heritage and all things we hold dear. It represents our most authentic self; it shows who we are when the mask is completely removed, how we emote, and if we are at peace with ourselves. This house contains information about what brings us a sense of emotional fulfillment, protection, and safety. The fourth house identifies how we define home literally in terms of our ideal environment, the area we'd like to live in, and the kind of house we'd like, and figuratively in terms of our family values and what comforts us. This house reveals a person's spiritual foundation or religious instincts (conservative or eclectic). This house is so important because even if everything else in your life is going well, you won't be completely happy unless the circumstances of your life are aligned with the qualities of the sign in your fourth house. The fourth house rules home, so it can speak of the connection we have to Mother Earth herself.

The esoteric significance of the fourth house deals with all things maternal, all things goddess, all things ancestral, and according to some, our attitude toward the Earth (the nurturer of all). I would even extend that to include how people generally perceive the experience and purpose of life on Earth as well. In other words, this house may reveal one's inclination toward the divine feminine or the divine masculine, how deeply one connects with their ancestral traditions, or what aspects of one's culture is emphasized or gravitated toward the most. For example, I have Cancer in the fourth house on my chart, so I am going to emphasize the ways my ancestors nurtured and cared for the people. Food, spirituality, and the arts are going to be of great interest. I also have Jupiter in the fourth house in Cancer, so that will further highlight my interest in my ancestors' religious and philosophical beliefs.

The Eighth House

The eighth house relates to Scorpio, the eighth sign of the zodiac. The natural rulers of the eighth house are the planet Mars and Pluto. The eighth house is the house of death, rebirth, mysteries, sacred sexuality, and the occult. It is the house of transformation. The eighth house rules a person's longevity, defeat, strife, sorrow, mental anxieties, worries, delays, scandals, and obstacles. It may indicate the circumstances surrounding the chart holder's death, including one's duration of life, manner of death, and whether death will come naturally or unnaturally, quickly, violently, or peacefully. The eighth house also speaks of bonding at the deepest level. The esoteric significance of this house deals with our attitude toward change in general and the ultimate change, which is death. It also reveals the true nature of our dark side, what it's capable of and how it operates—our criminal tendencies, bad habits, sexual problems, and addictions. In order to grow spiritually, it's absolutely essential for us to examine every aspect of who we are so we can make conscious decisions and create a personalized plan to enact change.

The Twelfth House

The twelfth house relates to Pisces, the twelfth sign of the zodiac, and the natural ruler of the twelfth house is the planet Jupiter. The twelfth house is the house of service to others, unity with God, secrets, compassion, limitations, psychic abilities, loss, misfortune, silent suffering, and hidden enemies. It also rules the imagination, the subconscious mind, creativity, and the arts. It represents what you have to let go in order to grow spiritually. It also indicates one's ability and comfort with letting go of materialism for the sake of spiritual development. This can be painful but is absolutely necessary in order to move on to the next stage of the soul's development.

The spiritual significance of the twelfth house deals with our attitude toward sacrifice. It is often indicative of our willingness to let go of thoughts or behaviors that no longer serve us and the manner by which we accomplish this.

The Signs in the Fourth House

Family, Home, Ancestors, and Suffering

THE FOURTH HOUSE, RELATED TO CANCER and the moon, is the house of our sense of home and traditions, of security and protection. It is also the house of our true, authentic self, revealing who we are under any facade. Other concerns that fall under this house are our emotional, physical, and spiritual well-being, as well as our lineage and lessons passed on from our ancestors.

✷✷✷

ARIES IN THE FOURTH HOUSE

Your Emotional Well-Being

People with Aries in the fourth house may have grown up in a volatile domestic environment or in a loud, crime-ridden neighborhood. Many people with this placement have borne witness to serious anger issues in the home, and possibly even physical or emotional abuse growing up.

Each imbalance here speaks of pain and hurt, and even abuse or anger deeply seeded in one's family tree. As a result of witnessing or participating in constant battle, you may be unnecessarily combative with others or lack compassion for whomever you perceive to be weak. In order to heal from this, you will have to make a practice of putting yourself in someone else's shoes before you dismiss their choices as cowardly or unchivalrous. Everyone doesn't have the same code and they shouldn't be expected to adhere to your standards.

Physical activity is very important to your health and happiness. Channel all of your fire into physical exercise! Doing so will be of tremendous benefit as you get older and you will appear much younger than you are. Remain active.

Your Spiritual Well-Being

It is imperative for you to be discerning about what you accept as spiritually or philosophically true. Aries is a fiery sign, so you have the tendency to charge ahead without reflecting on the implications or long-term consequences of what you say or do. It's perfectly fine to be a champion for truth and justice, but just make sure whatever ideology you're so passionate about is really in alignment with your core values.

Fourth house Aries should also beware of a tendency toward selfishness by ensuring that whatever you are fighting for is for the greater good. You will grow spiritually from living your life in this manner and by channeling all of your passion into transcending gross materialism.

Your Home

It's super important for those with Aries in the fourth house to invest their energy into improving their homes, so you will be very happy taking on a DIY project. It doesn't matter if you have experience or not. In fact, it's even better for you to venture outside of your comfort zone since Aries are not known to shy away from a challenge. You might even discover you have a real talent and interest in refurbishing things or woodworking. Not only will doing a DIY project bring you a sense of satisfaction because you built something yourself, but it could turn into a hobby or a new skill set to bring in extra money. Perhaps this will be the beginning of a lifelong love affair and give you something meaningful to do when you retire. Another perk is it can become a bonding opportunity for you and your family that doesn't involve being sedentary.

It would be a great idea for you to display your accomplishments around your home. It will bring you a sense of pride and encourage you to keep achieving. Consider a color scheme for your home in bold, powerful colors and patterns—the red or orange family would be therapeutic for you and help you maintain a happy, upbeat energy. Objects and furniture should be unfussy and well organized.

Aries in the fourth house people should be extra mindful not to permit unnecessary drama in the home, because things could get out of hand. The best way to accomplish this is to be transparent about what you expect from the people you live with. To keep things running smoothly, deal breakers, pet peeves, and solutions should be discussed before you move in with anyone. Also, learn to choose your battles wisely and try not to fly off the handle the moment something doesn't go your way.

Those with Aries in the fourth house usually like to get things done around the house and don't like to wait for others to help. As a result, they end up doing everything, become resentful, and then explode because others aren't pulling their weight, shocking their housemates because they seemed perfectly fine taking care of things on their own. So, to prevent an unpleasant situation, it would be best to delegate responsibilities in the home.

People with Aries in the fourth house usually have some form of leadership role in their families no matter their chronological age. While this is great, it would be wise to not be too aggressive about other people doing things your way. Pay attention when your relatives express concern about controlling behavior and remember the value of compromise. Keep in mind that the most effective leaders are receptive to wise counsel and reflect on the consequences of making hasty decisions. However, once a decision has been made, Aries shouldn't hesitate to act.

Lineage and Lessons

The lineage of those with Aries in the fourth house is most likely comprised of very strong-willed people who believed in the family sticking together through thick and thin. They also fought for what they believe in, even if it meant not fitting in or prolonged combat with others. These ideas were most likely passed down to you, which is why you should be clear about where you stand regarding life's major questions.

Psychic Influence

Those with Aries in their fourth house will not cling to traditional ideas, especially if they see flaws in their foundations. However, they may be too quick to debunk or divorce themselves from their parental or ancestral ways or knowledge. While it's great to be open to new ideas, make sure you give the mores and values you grew up with a chance. Make sure that you're not abandoning lessons of real value just because you're going through a phase or because it challenges you to think beyond a short-term desire or goal. Don't throw the baby out with the bathwater!

Due to this placement, you also have manifestation powers that are easily developed because it's an inherited talent from your ancestors. However, if you're not aware of this you might be missing an opportunity to live a better life and acquire more of what you want.

Creating Stronger Romantic Bonds

People with Aries in the fourth house would create the strongest romantic bond with a partner who respects their individuality and freedom. You need to be in a relationship with someone who isn't clingy and has an active social life and rewarding career independent of your relationship. This is absolutely necessary for you to feel like you can make moves without your partner relying on you as an all-encompassing source of meaning or amusement.

Those with Aries in the fourth house need a partner who is just as strong willed as they are or they will become frustrated and lose interest very quickly. Do yourself a favor and run, don't walk, if you meet people who need a lot of hand-holding or encouragement in order to do what they have to do. Aries don't mind being role models, but they require a confident lover in order to really make a connection, and it will be easier for you to create a strong romantic bond with a thick-skinned person who won't take your occasional outbursts personally.

★★★

TAURUS IN THE FOURTH HOUSE

Your Emotional Well-Being

You would be happiest if you have extra money to spend on gifts for yourself and your family. Invest in a well-stocked pantry. Your cabinets and refrigerator should never be empty. It will give you a subconscious sense of comfort if you are surrounded by abundance.

You should know exactly where you stand with everyone who lives under the same roof as you do. If there is any underlying tension with housemates, you need to resolve the issue or move on quickly.

Your Spiritual Well-Being

Security is important to you. You would be wise to seek security in every aspect of your domestic and financial life. You should always have a savings account. However, be careful not to become a scrooge or hyper materialistic. Resist the propaganda that all spiritual people have to be rebels who live on the edge—that's not for you, and that's okay!

To grow spiritually, you will have to consider not only your own needs but the needs of others in your community. Learn to find joy in service to others.

Your Home

A spacious home in close proximity to nature would be best for you. It would also be wise to consider if you'll still be comfortable living there when you're older. For example, do you have to walk up a hill or climb several flights of stairs, which may make it difficult for you to remain there once you become a senior? Consider this before you buy.

Your home should be filled with music and art and it should be a welcoming, fun place to be for yourself and others. Earth tones would be the best choice for your home but any shades in the green family would be equally soothing. Most importantly, your furniture should be super comfortable, stylish, and contemporary. *Everything* in your home—from eating utensils to bookcases—should be the best quality that you can afford. Even if house guests don't notice, you'll know you did your best, and this will give you a sense of pride.

Lineage and Lessons

Taurus in the fourth house people were most likely descended from "salt of the Earth" or business types with a deep connection to the land. There will be great spiritual benefits if you also seek such a connection with the Earth and her creatures. Try gardening.

Psychic Influence

Those with Taurus in the fourth house can have a strong effect on those around them, so they must be conscious of the influence they have on other people. It's important not to take advantage of this ability to persuade others. Be careful not to become dogmatic, and resist the urge to mock or bully others who disagree with your perspective on things.

Creating Stronger Romantic Bonds

People with Taurus in the fourth house would create the strongest romantic bond with a person who is equally committed to the success of the relationship. They need to know that they will get a return on the time and energy they are investing in someone else. When their lover's intentions aren't clear and their goals as a couple are vague, it creates distance.

Choose a partner who appreciates sensuality and affectionate displays, someone who enjoys a candlelight dinner, soft music, and a glass of wine just as much as you do. Your partner can have a freaky side, but you don't like being smutty or inappropriate, so make sure your partner understands the difference.

Make sure your preference for ease doesn't lead to toxic passivity. There are times when confrontation is necessary.

✶✶✶

GEMINI IN THE FOURTH HOUSE

Your Emotional Well-Being

People with Gemini in their fourth house are happiest when they are actively pursuing knowledge. You would be happiest if you find time to do research, read, or take classes relative to topics of interest. For example, consider doing genealogy research on your family tree. People with this placement usually enjoy uncovering details about their family's past. In fact, it can be quite a life-changing endeavor for them.

There is a tendency for people with this placement to lament "being born in the wrong era" because they believe people were deeper or smarter in days gone by. Sometimes these feelings arise because they are disconnected from contemporary life or the way society functions. While there is certainly much to criticize about our generation, it would serve those with Gemini in the fourth house to acknowledge that there is no time in history where people didn't romanticize "the good old days." You were born exactly when you were supposed to be. So don't waste that brilliant mind looking backward but consider how you can integrate what you appreciate about bygone eras into the present.

Try not to indulge all of your interests at once to prevent burn out, lack of productivity, and missed opportunities due to flightiness. Resist the urge to abandon things as soon as there is a slight lag. Concentrate! Your lack of focus and consistency may eventually make you feel empty because you never really mastered anything but settled on being a jack of all trades.

Your Spiritual Well-Being

It would be of tremendous benefit for those with Gemini in the fourth house to travel for the express purpose of gaining spiritual insight. Visit national and international sacred sites and holy places. This will benefit you immensely if you resist the urge to simply collect facts about the places you visit and really attempt to connect with the essence of these special places.

People with Gemini in the fourth house have an incredible analytical ability that would be best used to identify the similarities and interconnectedness of different cultures and ways of life. In order to grow spiritually, seek the unity of all things and the divine in the mundane. Change the world not by seeking salvation or enlightenment via the experiences of others but by realizing things for yourself.

Your Home

The décor of your home should reflect your intellectual interests. Consider how you transmit knowledge in your home via the art and items on display. What are the conscious and subconscious messages you're transmitting to guests and those dwelling in your home? This matters more than color schemes for you. You would be most happy with bold, eclectic furnishings, and inspirational quotes placed throughout the home may inspire you.

Lineage and Lessons

People with Gemini in the fourth house are most likely descended from intellectuals, journalists, musicians, researchers, record keepers, accountants, writers, or other "bookish" types. Maintain spiritual health and balance by remaining open to new ideas and points of view that may be different than your own.

Psychic Influence

Geminis in the fourth house tend to have a way with words like no one else, and people will be affected by what you say and how you say it. They are used to people telling them how something they said changed their lives, for positive or negative. Use your words wisely!

You've probably noticed your ability to comprehend complex subjects and difficult concepts better than others. You may also have the capacity for understanding the perspectives of opposites. Use your natural ability as a "devil's advocate" to squash arguments and bring people together. Use your wit and legendary sense of humor to deescalate situations.

Creating Stronger Romantic Bonds

Geminis in the fourth house may have issues with making commitments, so don't agree to a monogamous relationship unless you're absolutely sure you're ready. Be sure that person is someone you can talk to; you will not be able to really bond with a romantic partner unless you find conversation intellectually stimulating. It doesn't matter how kind partners are, how much money they have, or how good they look . . . you will not be satisfied without that mental connection. Sapiosexuals often have this placement.

It's very important that your relationships permit you to express yourself freely and openly or you will feel insecure, burdened, and unhappy.

CANCER IN THE FOURTH HOUSE

Your Emotional Well-Being

Those with the sign of Cancer in the fourth house would be wise to surround themselves with people whom they know, beyond a doubt, have their best interests at heart. There is absolutely no place for ambiguity, or feelings of instability, insecurity, and lovelessness will steadily increase.

Become more comfortable with the inevitability of loss as a natural part of life. It's a hard pill to swallow, but eventually all things come to an end. Sometimes people we care about move on, move away, or pass away, and you will have to learn to make peace with that reality or risk falling completely apart when these situations occur. When they do, practice self-care, seek help from friends and family, or contact a mental health professional if you require additional support. Avoid isolation when you feel depressed or things can get out of hand.

Avoid the tendency to disconnect from others because you have been hurt in the past or because you're afraid of getting hurt. It's okay to be cautious, but don't fall into the trap of masking pessimism or negative self-talk as sense and sensibility.

Don't be a worrywart. Consider the pros and cons of every choice, make a decision, and have faith that things will work out for the greater good.

Your Spiritual Well-Being

Fourth house Cancerians must learn to love themselves unconditionally. The only way to do this is to be patient with yourself and become more confident in your ability to overcome any challenges you may encounter. Learn to trust the universe and believe that you will be divinely guided.

It would be wise for you to learn to observe your emotions without judging them or acting on them. Every feeling doesn't warrant an immediate response; become accustomed to acknowledging your feelings without being so quick to identify with a particular one.

Situations may often make us feel a range of different emotions, so give yourself some time to think things through to avoid any unnecessary outbursts.

If you identify with love and act from a place of love you will find that you will get more of what you want out of life. This is true for everyone, but is especially true for you.

Your Home

You will be blessed when you feed people, so get prepared to host dinner parties for people you care about. Invest in a kitchen and dining area that you can be proud of.

The décor of your home should be cozy, antique, or nostalgic. Consider displaying memorabilia, artwork, or objects related to your culture, religion, or ancestry; souvenirs from the places you've visited; and beautifully framed pictures of loved ones. The color scheme should be cool and soothing. Lighter shades of blue, silver, or pearly white would be best, and you may also want to invest in an aquarium or artwork that includes calm water scenes.

Consider placing protective symbols near the front and back door or anywhere else intruders could possibly enter the home. These symbols can be big, small, or written in invisible ink, as long as you know they're there.

Lineage and Lessons

The lineage of those with Cancer in the fourth house most likely consists of homemakers, cooks, caretakers for children or the elderly, nurses, midwives, counselors, empaths, or any profession that involves nurturing others. These ancestors emphasized the importance of maintaining strong family bonds and selfless action. The family passed down these lessons, and it is highly likely that you have a very strong intuition and sense of responsibility to your community.

Psychic Influence

You have a very strong intuition, almost to the point of psychic ability. You often use your talent to help and provide support for others.

Creating Stronger Romantic Bonds

Cancers in the fourth house would do best in safe, predictable, monogamous relationships. Your partner should not be emotionally unavailable or fearful of emotional intimacy or you will certainly get hurt. Your partner should be protective and dedicated and revel in all of your attention. It would be best to date someone who won't mind cuddling at home most of the time and doesn't mind splurging on dinner at your favorite restaurants, or it may become a serious source of contention.

Ensure that your partner is family oriented or is willing to become part of your clan once you've both decided to make things official. It would be almost impossible for you to feel secure or comfortable with anyone that doesn't get along with your kin or close friends or who doesn't like or want children.

Cheating will make you feel really, really bad. Don't do it. Express how you feel about infidelity to anyone that expresses interest in being in a serious relationship with you. Be certain that a potential partner understands what you consider disloyal or inappropriate behavior to prevent misunderstandings, unnecessary conflict, or a premature breakup. Do not agree to couple with anyone who disagrees or expresses annoyance with your perspective regarding matters of the heart.

✳✳✳

LEO IN THE FOURTH HOUSE

Your Emotional Well-Being

Those with Leo in the fourth house would benefit from learning more about the artistic legacy of their ancestors regardless of genre. They will feel empowered and feel a tremendous sense of pride from learning about their accomplishments, which will in turn increase their self-esteem.

As hard as it may seem, it's not all about you. Consider the needs of others and pay attention when people are accusing you of being domineering or self-serving. Rather than immediately denying these accusations, reflect on these incidents to ensure that there isn't some truth to it.

You would benefit immensely from spending more time outdoors, especially during the daylight hours. In addition, it's important that you have at least one goal or mission that you believe in 100 percent; channel all of that Leonine energy into making your dream a reality.

Your Spiritual Well-Being

Low-vibration Leos in the fourth house pride themselves on their ability to dominate or manipulate others. High-vibration Leos in the fourth house pride themselves on their discipline and self-mastery.

Recognize that a good leader respects the fact that people grow and evolve at their own pace, in their own time. Don't resort to bullying or ridicule to force people to agree with you. The source of your courage should be based on strong moral values and the desire to do the right thing for the benefit of others, not anger or pride.

Your Home

It's best for Leos in the fourth house to own wherever they live, so you might want to look into buying a home or a condo. Make sure that you're proud of the neighborhood and the home you dwell in. Make sure the artwork and objects on display communicate power and wealth, as your home should be your castle. Appropriate color schemes involve deep reds and jewel tones. The areas where you entertain guests should be as impressive and lavish as you can afford.

There should be a room or area in your home that is completely yours, preferably a space dedicated to some form of creative self-expression.

Lineage and Lessons

The lineage of those with Leo in the fourth house most likely consists of performing artists, aristocrats or community leaders, managers, or people involved in real estate or agriculture. They emphasized the importance of fortitude, courage, and good leadership skills and passed those lessons on to you. It is highly likely you have inherited the power to persuade and influence others without even trying.

Psychic Influence

Pay attention to what you highlight about your personality to others, because they are always watching what you do and how you do it. What you project into the world often becomes a reality, so be careful what energy you put out into the universe.

Whatever you focus most of your energy on will most likely affect the souls of all those that participate in any projects you're working on. Be responsible.

Creating Stronger Romantic Bonds

You need to feel appreciated and even put on a pedestal by your lover. Lovers should be more comfortable with giving than receiving on every level. Admit this and seek such people.

Refuse "pissing contests" with your significant other. Choose someone who admires people who know what they want and are willing to do whatever it takes to get it. A significant other who is jealous of your ambition or accomplishments would be a disaster and the relationship will end very badly.

★★★

VIRGO IN THE FOURTH HOUSE

Your Emotional Well-Being

People with Virgo in the fourth house would be much happier if they could learn to accept the world as it is. Challenge notions of what you think a perfect world looks like; it may be perfect to you, but to others your vision may be just as problematic as you think this reality is. So whose perception is right and whose perception is wrong? Just live the way you want to live and let it go.

Be kinder to yourself and others when they make mistakes. Life is complex, and we're all trying to figure things out.

Your Spiritual Well-Being

Stop minimizing the importance of making progress, no matter how small. Learn to enjoy the whole journey by celebrating all-sized victories and daily blessings. Try retelling something that went wrong as your favorite comedian would describe the situation during a stand-up routine. Learn to laugh at yourself.

Don't forget to remain engaged in the world beyond material pursuits. When was the last time you watched the sunrise?

Beware of imposing your beliefs about how you think things should be done. Reserve your high standards for yourself or you risk alienating the people you claim to care about. You have a talent for knowing exactly what needs to be done to improve a situation, but let others come to you for advice. No one likes a know-it-all.

Your Home

The home of someone with Virgo in their fourth house should be clean, sanitary, and highly organized, with everything in its proper place. Keeping things neat and tidy is about more than an attractive presentation—it is absolutely essential to your comfort. Your home should run like a well-oiled machine, and it should be filled with appliances and gadgets that allow you to make more efficient use of your time. Convenience is key.

The décor of your home should be refined and minimalist. A few low-maintenance plants, like bonsai, aloe, cactus, ferns, or eucalyptus, would be both ornamental and therapeutic to have around. A color scheme worthy of consideration would be lighter shades of gray, sand, or salmon. If you want to add a touch of color, then try bright yellow flowers in earthy wooden, clay, or ceramic vases throughout the house.

Be discerning about who you allow into your home. If you don't have your own place, then change that as soon as you are able to so you can control the energy in your environment and who is permitted to visit.

Lineage and Lessons

The lineage of fourth house Virgos is most likely comprised of mechanics, health care providers, nutritionists, scientists, or professionals involved in any work that requires precision or attention to detail. They emphasized the importance of logic, hard work, conservative values, and the importance of doing one's best, and passed those lessons on to you. It is highly likely that you have the ability to give expert-level advice and know how to find a solution to complex problems. You are able to see things others don't see because your mind has surgical precision.

Psychic Influence

You are a natural problem solver and that's great! But beware of people who may pick up on your desire to fix them and end up using you.

Creating Stronger Romantic Bonds

Make sure your lover meets your hygiene expectations and has dietary habits that you accept and respect. Don't date anyone that is unable to accept constructive criticism, or things won't work out.

Avoid the tendency to remain tight lipped about how you feel, or your partner may begin to feel neglected. Open up.

It's important for your family to like your partner, so make sure that partner is already good enough to meet them. If you have to try to convince your lover to do a make-over in any way to be fit to meet your family, that may breed resentment. Resist the urge to fall in love with a person's potential.

Choose an optimist for long-term relationships to balance your pessimistic or perfectionist tendencies.

✳✳✳

LIBRA IN THE FOURTH HOUSE

Your Emotional Well-Being

There is a tendency for those with Libra in the fourth house to constantly compare themselves to others, which can wreak havoc on a person's self-esteem. It is imperative for you to cultivate a positive self-image that won't change with the ups and downs of fortune. You should love yourself whether you have one dollar or one million dollars!

Your Spiritual Well-Being

Recognize that no matter how objective you believe yourself to be, you are not. Everyone is a product of their life experiences and those experiences affect how we perceive the world and ourselves.

Learn how to deal with conflict in a healthy way instead of avoiding the issue.

Do what you have to do to be comfortable in your own skin—stop trying to keep up with the Joneses. Pursue occupations and hobbies that you find respectable and that bring you a sense of peace.

Don't wait forever for "the perfect time" to do something you really want to do, because, more often than not, it doesn't exist. That doesn't mean you have to be careless, but learn to take a risk when necessary.

Your Home

People with Libra in the fourth house need their home to be a beautiful refuge that they can't wait to retreat to after a long day. Your home should be filled with beautiful things (but not to the point of appearing cluttered). Shades of blue or pastels with light-colored furniture and a fluffy pet to curl up next to is the way to go.

If you live with other people, make sure you address any grievances that may arise right away. It's unhealthy for anyone to endure negative energy at home, but for you it's ten times worse. Resist the urge to stick your head in the sand while praying for the problem to resolve itself.

Lineage and Lessons

The lineage of fourth house Librans most likely consists of beauticians, seamstresses, lawyers, artists, diplomats, hoteliers, or any other profession that requires intellect and creativity. They emphasized the importance of charm, grace, and maintaining a good reputation and passed those lessons on to you. It is highly likely that you have the ability to put people at ease when no one else can get control of a volatile situation. People respect you as a voice of reason and tend to listen to what you have to say.

Psychic Influence

Those with Libra in the fourth house have the ability to bring people together in a spirit of celebration. Use your wit and charm to spread joy to everyone who crosses your path instead of using it just to get what you want. Whenever you need to make a certain move, throw a party with a carefully curated guest list, with the intention of attracting the hook-up or information you're seeking. The answer will appear and will be well worth the expense of all that wine and cheese.

Creating Stronger Romantic Bonds

People with Libra in their fourth house would really connect with a partner who believes in traditional ideas about love and romance.

Admit to potential partners from the beginning that you care about anniversaries and old-fashioned courting rituals so you don't feel deprived or disappointed. If a person you're considering dating expresses any cynical or dismissive attitudes regarding this, immediately count your losses and move on. You won't be happy with that partner in the long run even if you've convinced yourself that it's not a big deal now.

If a potential partner expresses disinterest in a serious relationship, you may want to re-evaluate whether you should continue. You want to be in love and shouldn't waste time trying to convince partners they should, too. Make sure your love values, expectations, and intensity levels are compatible before pairing up.

✳✳✳

SCORPIO IN THE FOURTH HOUSE

Your Emotional Well-Being

Those with Scorpio in the fourth house may hold a grudge against their families due to the discovery of deep, dark secrets or an incident of betrayal that tore the family apart. Cut off whomever needs to be cut off or move away, but it's critical that you take note of how these incidents affected you. Be careful not to allow your bitterness or resentment to ruin your future.

Don't try to solve everyone else's problems unless you have found solutions to yours first. It's exactly what flight attendants tell us about making sure we put on our own oxygen masks before attempting to assist our neighbors.

Become comfortable with change if you aren't already. You've probably experienced a lot of transformations regarding your home life, and that may continue.

Your Spiritual Well-Being

Heal your wounds so that you can learn to trust again.

Consider the possible consequences of putting any plans for revenge in motion and be prepared to live with the outcome, whatever that may be.

Your Home

Make sure that you trust whomever you live with enough to express your vulnerability. You're so used to playing your cards close to the chest that your home must be a safe space for you to be exactly who you are.

You probably don't care so much what your house looks like, since you live mostly inside your head. If you do get around to decorating, don't hide your style. It's highly likely that your décor will shock visitors to your home, but don't let that prevent you from choosing dark or risqué artwork, black or red walls, or a rather odd indoor fountain, or transforming your study into a replica of the bat cave. It would be ideal for you to have a private room or space where you can quietly reflect.

Lineage and Lessons

The lineage of people with Scorpio in the fourth house most likely consists of in the military or were detectives, spies, occultists, researchers, mental health professionals, shamans, engineers, scientists, bill collectors, or professionals involved in any work that required unflappability and risk-taking. They emphasized the importance of courage, strength, perseverance, cunning, and going beyond the surface of things and passed those lessons on to you. It is highly likely that you have the ability to perceive when others are not who they present themselves to be, and you may even exhibit advanced psychic abilities without effort.

Psychic Influence

People can sense your power. Become aware of how your energy may invoke fear, confusion, or awe in some people so you'll be better equipped to manage situations more effectively.

Those with Scorpio in the fourth house tend to complain about receiving too much information and maybe personal details from people they just met. Strangers often feel comfortable telling them their deepest, darkest secrets, especially pertaining to things that happened to them or the freaky or taboo things they used to do in the past.

Creating Stronger Romantic Bonds

Don't even bother dating someone who doesn't desire a deep, intense emotional connection as much as you do. It won't work.

Let all potential partners know exactly what your deal breakers are, and let them know that the biggest one is being disloyal or dishonest. Do you even have any others?

✶✶✶

SAGITTARIUS IN THE FOURTH HOUSE

Your Emotional Well-Being

Resist the tendency to dismiss your feelings in favor of rattling off platitudes to avoid dealing with pain or disappointment. Try not to tell lies—it bothers you.

Stop casting pearls before swine. You are wise and possess amazing insights; save them for people who will be appreciative. Likewise, learn how to accept a compliment without attempting to minimize yourself. Just say thank you. Think before you speak. Make sure that the message you're attempting to transmit is the same message that's being received by whomever you're communicating with. This could prevent a lot of drama . . . which, of course, you absolutely hate.

Your Spiritual Well-Being

Fourth house Sagittarians need to be wary of violating their moral or ethical ideals, or they will suffer a sense of deep shame and regret. Keep it real, adhering to your highest standards.

Create a life that permits you as much freedom as possible to pursue what genuinely interests you, and encourage those around you to broaden their horizons as well. Share your knowledge freely without expecting anything in return, and you'll receive blessings.

Your Home

People with Sagittarius in the fourth house should bring the outdoors indoors by blanketing their house with plants and flowers. It will bring a sense of peace and well-being on a subconscious level. Exposure to a lot of natural light is very important as well.

You have a fondness for foreign people and cultures, so you might want to reflect that in your décor by choosing an exotic theme or by displaying artifacts from your travels. Think about a purple, orange, or royal blue color scheme.

Consider investing in a mobile home or occasionally renting an RV to satisfy your wanderlust.

Lineage and Lessons

The lineage of those with Sagittarius in the fourth house is most likely comprised of in the travel and tourism industry, marketers, scholars, judges, administrators, clergy, ambassadors, publishers, or professionals involved in any work that required adventure and a depth of highly specialized knowledge. They emphasized the importance of exploration, morality, or embracing change, and passed those lessons on to you. It is highly likely that you have the ability to see beyond the surface of things without effort.

Psychic Influence

Sagittarius is one of the friendly signs, but someone with a placement in the fourth house may tend to be socially awkward and offend others because of something they said without meaning to. This can breed hidden enemies.

Creating Stronger Romantic Bonds

Make sure that all potential mates understand that you don't like to be pinned down or avalanched with expectations. You require someone who is totally comfortable seeing how things go, as opposed to a lover who is constantly pressing you to make a commitment. If monogamy isn't for you or isn't for you at a particular time, it's important for you to admit to being polyamorous.

Sagittarians tend to fizzle out in the romance rather quickly, so make sure you make a conscious decision to show affection to your partner even after the novelty has worn off.

✱✱✱

CAPRICORN IN THE FOURTH HOUSE

Your Emotional Well-Being

The tendency to be stubborn and resistant to change all the time can be a problem for fourth house Capricorns. Resist it! Instead of dismissing a new idea or method right out, consider how it might actually be helpful or more effective than the way you do things now. The conscious effort to challenge yourself will yield more of the results you're seeking.

Don't get so caught up in the grind that you forget to eat nutritious, well-balanced meals and to exercise. Your physical body still has needs even if you would prefer to keep working.

Your Spiritual Well-Being

The most important lesson for you is learning to manage that inner voice that whispers pessimistic or abusive thoughts to you. Don't allow perfectionism to ruin your happiness.

Never seek validation or proof of your relevance from external sources. You're already important! A certificate, diploma, or initiation may be useful for navigating or accessing certain spaces, but don't forget that it has nothing to do with true inner power.

Your Home

Those with Capricorn in their fourth house would thrive in conservatively decorated homes with traditional, sturdy leather furniture. Consider a brown, navy, or dark green color scheme with adjustable lighting. Try to get a house or apartment with a beautiful view.

Invest in a home office so you have a place to work where you won't be disturbed. You know how much you hate being interrupted when you're working on something.

Lineage and Lessons

The lineage of people with Capricorn in the fourth house most likely consists of antiquarians, businessmen, house flippers, scientists, electricians, geologists, auctioneers, or professionals involved in any work that requires great organizational skills, patience, and consistency. They emphasized the importance of being reliable, detail-oriented, and sober-minded and passed those lessons on to you. It is highly likely that you have way more self-discipline than others would be comfortably capable of.

Psychic Influence

People will tend to see you as an authority figure, and they may or may not like you because of that. Whether they like you or not depends on whether they have respect or disdain for those who they perceive as being higher than them. When people feel small, they can feel jealous; when people feel jealous, they begin to covet. You may attract many "frenemies," so be careful.

Creating Stronger Romantic Bonds

You would be most compatible with someone who values your ambition and sober planning. A "free spirit" type who keeps nagging you to be less practical will eventually become a drag. Even though public displays of affection may not be your thing, don't underestimate the impact of occasionally expressing your passion for your partner in front of other people. It doesn't have to be crass or distasteful, just a simple gesture will suffice. Lighten up a little.

If your significant other offends, annoys, or hurts you, resist the urge to silently hold a grudge. If forgivable, then forgive; if it isn't, then just break up.

✦✦✦

AQUARIUS IN THE FOURTH HOUSE

Your Emotional Well-Being

You're investigative, curious, and extremely active mentally. Your thinking mind rarely, if ever, stops. You need to learn how to relax and when to shut down, as your brain can become overactive, especially at night.

Fourth house Aquarians are humanitarians at heart and will spend a lot of time trying to convince others that we have more similarities than differences. However, you may become discouraged if your sound arguments for unity are continuously ignored. Don't waste your time trying to convince other people that they need to evolve. Instead, lead by example. You may be surprised by how many previously unrelenting people admit that you were right all along. Show, don't tell.

Your Spiritual Well-Being

You want to live life on your own terms, but before you can do that you must first be clear about what you really want. You'll also have to consider how far you'll go and who or what you're willing to sacrifice to get it. Sacrifice is unavoidable.

Your Home

Your home should have a futuristic feel. While years of science fiction books and movies have programmed us to believe that the future is minimalist with chrome and glass accents, that doesn't have to be how it looks! That's someone else's vision of the future and you don't have to agree with that. What would *you* like the future world to look like? Feel like? That's the vision that you should bring to life.

Lineage and Lessons

The lineage of people with Aquarius in their fourth house is most likely comprised of political activists, professors, entertainers, photographers, nurses, astronomers or astrologers, diviners, philanthropists, or professionals involved in any work that requires deep thought and creativity. They emphasized the importance of being independent-minded and innovative and passed those lessons on to you. It is highly likely that you have the ability to read people's minds and can accurately predict what they're going to say or do next without much effort.

Psychic Influence

You dance to the beat of your own drum and that might be considered a threat to more conservative types. You may make people uncomfortable with your unconventional views, especially if you criticize their religious or political ideologies.

Creating Stronger Romantic Bonds

Fourth house Aquarians need a lot of personal space, so make sure to not hook up with anyone whose clinginess or dependency exceeds your comfort level.

It's critical for you to have partners who are comfortable with change and won't be disturbed when you're not exactly the same person they met just six months earlier. They should also be open to your ideas and unafraid of changing their perspective.

✶✶✶

PISCES IN THE FOURTH HOUSE

Your Emotional Well-Being

Be vigilant about managing stress because it could easily begin to manifest as a physical condition. Resist the urge to eat or drink excessively when you feel hurt or disappointed.

You need people to talk to about your feelings, so don't hesitate to rely on your family and friends. If for some reason you don't have people in your life to confide in, you might want to consider getting a therapist or joining an online community for support.

Your Spiritual Well-Being

Everyone knows that being judgmental is not your thing, but don't be a fool either! If you meet someone and you see red flags, don't ignore them because you feel bad. Be kind to yourself and your future first. Don't let the fears or insecurities of others prevent you from pursuing your dreams or it will haunt you forever.

As someone with Pisces in your fourth house, loyalty and trust are super important to you. Your spiritual well-being would be improved immensely by ensuring that the people closest to you are 100 percent invested in your success and happiness.

As an empath, it is important to make sure you aren't holding on to what you may pick up from other people. Water is key. Take spiritual baths to cleanse your aura of any psychic debris you may have picked up, and bathe with sea salt whenever you feel depressed or unmotivated.

Your Home

Your home must be a place of peace, your own personal fantasy land. More than anything else, fourth house Pisceans need to be able to recharge and daydream, so you need a room or space for you to be by yourself. Consider including images of water in the artwork displayed or investing in a beautiful aquarium or an indoor fountain. If you are religious or follow a spiritual path, then you would benefit from having imagery or symbols of your beliefs around for inspiration and comfort.

Lineage and Lessons

The lineage of people with Pisces in their fourth house most likely consists of in the navy or coast guard, fisherman, mystics, therapists, ship captains, artists, religious leaders, social workers, sommeliers, musicians, or professionals involved in any work that requires sensitivity, extraordinary depth, and a vivid imagination. They emphasized the importance of trying to make the world a better place and helping others, and passed that on to you. It is highly likely that many of the things you dream about actually come true, and you're used to déjà vu.

Psychic Influence

You are a natural healer and empath, and other people can sense it. You know how to make people feel better, but that can also open you up to psychic debris, which you will need to cleanse. Create boundaries, respect them, and make other people respect them. Protect your magic.

Creating Stronger Romantic Bonds

It's important that you feel valued in your relationships, so stay clear of lovers with a wandering eye or who are in any way less devoted to you then you are to them. You have a broad, open mind and you love to share your insights with others. Therefore it would be best to find someone who doesn't mind having intense, philosophical discussions on a regular basis.

You feel very deeply, so sometimes you can take things the wrong way. Try to focus on the intention behind what was said even if the delivery wasn't exactly to your liking. Unless your significant other is just a jerk, most likely she or he did not intend to hurt you but was just trying to get you to focus.

Avoid the tendency to "space out" so much that your partner begins to feel neglected because you're always in your own head. You can prevent this by creating a "dreamscape" for two every now and then. Watch the sunrise or sunset together, or send poems expressing how you feel.

The Signs in the Eighth House

Sex, Death, Secret Powers,
and Transformation

THE EIGHTH HOUSE RELATES TO SCORPIO, the eighth sign of the zodiac. The traditional ruler of this house is Mars and, later, Pluto. The eighth house is the house of sex, death, personal transformation, and secret powers. It is the house of hidden potential.

This house contains information about a person's emotional and spiritual perception of sex. It reveals our expectations for more serious committed relationships. The eighth house also identifies the qualities we must master in order to reach a new level of spiritual growth. It is very likely that we won't like the qualities of the sign in the eighth house because adopting those qualities will require us to destroy our self-image. The more invested we are in remaining the same, the more we will be irritated by or fearful of what lies in the eighth house, because of its power to end our old way of being. The eighth house involves the soul-level changes we go through in a lifetime.

✯✯✯

ARIES IN THE EIGHTH HOUSE

Sexual Intimacy

Study the art of making love. Watch videos, take courses, or invest in books that explain different techniques on how to give pleasure to your partner. *The Kama Sutra* is the most well-known, but there are many others to explore, such as the *Ananga Ranga, Sexual Kung Fu, Kunyaza, The Perfumed Garden of Sensual Delight, The Return of the Old Man to His Youth, T of Lady Purity,* and *The Golden Lotus,* to name a few. Challenge yourself, because it will make you an even more dynamic lover.

If you're not aware that you would be into rough sex, you are— even if you don't know it yet! The more passion, the better. However, beware of the tendency to start arguments with your lover just for the purpose of having hot make-up sex.

Sometimes people with this placement want to have the final say regarding how quickly a relationship develops and may become belligerent if things are not going their way. They need to recognize that some people need a bit more time before they jump into situations feet first. Your lovers should be told up front that you are territorial, protective, bossy, and intense, just in case any of those traits are deal breakers. Failure to mention how assertive you are now could backfire later, after the novelty of the relationship wears off.

Your Elevated Self-Image

Those with Aries in the eighth house are sensitive to power dynamics between people and prefer to be dominant in that regard. You already have the ability to influence others, which is why you get annoyed when people don't do things your way. Study how to increase your powers of persuasion.

Aries in the eighth house is a "hero's journey" placement, which makes an individual's search for truth mandatory in order to grow and become more confident. In most hero's journey tales, heroes are invited to embark on a quest or feel compelled to do so. The point is, they usually make a conscious decision to leave their comfort zone in order to complete a sacred or important mission. Once they have accepted the challenge, they are also usually given, intuit, or make a list of what is needed and/or who needs to be contacted to increase their chances of success. The road ahead is often fraught with danger, so it is in their best interest to be as prepared as they can. They have faith, but they are clear about the stakes and don't take unnecessary risks. Avoid blind faith.

Your Secret Power

Our third eye is located at the pineal gland, which is a tiny gland shaped like a pinecone. It is near the hypothalamus and pituitary gland and is considered to be the source of our intuition, imagination, and connectedness to all sentient beings. It is said that when people have an open third eye, they are more compassionate and may have the ability to perform miracles.

Transformations and Endings

The most important thing that people with Aries in their eighth house could learn is that rage is a secondary emotion, often brought forward in order to sublimate pain or disappointment, and if they could process those first, it would change their lives. They tend to feel more comfortable expressing anger, but they will build stronger relationships with others if they turn down the volume and train themselves to talk things out in a calm, rational way.

You would do best to live by a code that informs the manner by which you end any kind of a relationship, be it professional or romantic. This will prevent you from making unnecessary mistakes because you got carried away. For example, a samurai was expected to approach life in a particular manner in order to be considered a true samurai. You, too, would benefit from adopting or creating your own code of honor to guide you in making decisions.

Get in the habit of reevaluating what you need when you find yourself feeling uninspired or restless. It's very important for those with Aries in the eighth house to always have a clear, well-defined spiritual mission or ideal to pursue. You are a role model, whether you want to be or not, so never underestimate your ability to affect change in the lives of others.

Avoid the urge to rush gestational periods of your life. While it is not recommended that you immediately act on changes you feel you need to make, it doesn't mean that you won't achieve the results you are seeking—they will just take time to come to fruition. Situations need time to ripen.

People with this placement tend to rehash situations and waste valuable energy on petty conflicts and inconveniences. This is an awful waste of your passion! If your instincts tell you that whatever drama you're engaged in isn't worth it, then disengage immediately. Stop focusing on how the other person or people interpret your retreat; that's irrelevant, because you're doing it for you.

Aries in this house indicates that the transition from this life may come suddenly or involve violence. There is also a possibility of death by fire, smoke inhalation, or head trauma.

✶✶✶

TAURUS IN THE EIGHTH HOUSE

Sexual Intimacy

Eighth house Taureans are extremely sensual and enjoy incorporating candles, incense, aphrodisiacs, and scented oils or lotions into the sexual experience. They should try to integrate the power of sound into their sexual encounters. That could mean setting the mood with the right music or, even better, the sound of your voice. Seduce your lover by singing to them or reading erotic poetry prior to being intimate and you will mesmerize. Taureans want to stimulate all five senses of their lover and also want to experience the same. They are genuinely appreciative of long-term partners who maintain their appearance and all efforts to keep things interesting in the bedroom.

Virtue is inextricably linked to sexual intimacy for a person with this placement, whether they are aware of it or not. Therefore it is strongly recommended that you choose sexual partners who are virtuous according to how you see the world. Otherwise, you will run the risk of feeling drained.

Women with this placement may have sex in exchange for material gifts or comfort and are the most likely to have a sugar daddy. Men with Taurus in the eighth house are promised blessings if they are very generous to their significant others.

Your Elevated Self-Image

When eighth house Taureans retain an attitude of gratitude and appreciation for what they have, regardless of how little, then they will begin to operate on a much higher frequency. This will be a challenge because of the desire to "live in luxury," but, once this message has been thoroughly internalized, their self-image and entire life will become truly beautiful. At this level, the stability is not in the acquisition or pursuit of material possessions, but in connecting to the imperfect perfection of life on Earth.

Release the fear of not being or having enough. Most likely, you are and you do, but your constant worrying may have convinced you to believe differently.

This placement indicates that it would be wise to make sure that you fully comprehend the purpose of whatever you teach to others.

Your Secret Power

People with Taurus in the eighth house have the ability to commune with elemental Earth spirits and work wonders with plant-based magic and herbology. They should look into forest bathing as a way to connect, refresh, and recharge.

Some people with this placement have the ability to manifest what they need when they need it, as long as they make a conscious effort to do so.

Transformations and Endings

People with this placement can be very slow at implementing necessary changes and would benefit from supportive friends who encourage them to push on when it's time to finally make a move. You need to be careful that you don't wait until situations become dire to make the changes you need to make. Once you realize that something needs to be handled, devise an efficient, well-thought-out plan to get things done.

Eighth house Taureans may pass away this lifetime as a result of an illness related to overindulgence in sweets or rich, fatty foods. Death comes slowly but peacefully.

✳✳✳

GEMINI IN THE EIGHTH HOUSE

Sexual Intimacy

Eighth house Geminis should consider adding more spontaneity and risqué fun to their sex lives to prevent boredom. Keep the passion alive in your relationship by not having a fixed sex schedule and periodically trying to have sex in unorthodox places. Perfect your oral sex skills since you have the predisposition to be a legend at it, and be sure to choose a partner who won't be weirded out if you decide to get kinky or experimental in the bedroom.

Communication is one of Gemini's keywords, so don't be shy about sending sexy texts to your lover or talking dirty during sex. Also, given your propensity to ask probing questions and insist on knowing everyone's backstory, it would be best if whoever you're dating has a "my life is an open book" attitude.

Eighth house Geminis may take a long time to trust someone with their heart, so deep, penetrating intimacy may take some time. Potential love interests should know and accept this from the start.

Your Elevated Self-Image

People with Gemini in their eighth house will grow exponentially when they realize that their considerable intellectual prowess was not meant to be used to dominate, manipulate, or intimidate others but, instead, to elevate them.

Your Secret Power

People who have Gemini in their eighth house have the ability to become extraordinary astrologers or metaphysicians.

Your wit and cleverness are a superpower when refined. People may not notice all that is going on under the surface, as you are the personification of the saying "still waters run deep." Consider taking up chess, go, or another game to keep you sharp.

Transformations and Endings

You have the temperament to be able to handle the chaos that comes with growth and transformation. As long as you are clear about why the changes are necessary, you'll be totally fine. Stop being scared of the dark—confront your fears.

Try not to suppress your darker or more risqué thoughts all of the time. They are just as worthy as all the others and may even attract someone interesting whom you never would have met had you not had the courage to speak your mind. You already respect people who speak their truth and freely share their ideas. How about becoming one of them?

By contrast, it is also important that you don't underestimate the usefulness of small talk. More than likely, you prefer more probing, intense discussions, but sometimes some of the deepest conversations may begin with a comment about the weather.

You will grow spiritually if you sacralize the learning process. In other words, don't just gather information so that you can say you know something. Instead, seek to understand what you learn and look for ways to apply that knowledge to your everyday life. Your intellect should serve your expansion as a person, as a being.

Avoid co-dependency situations, either as the giver or the receiver. These kinds of relationships can, for example, result in the manipulation of a financially weaker person by the breadwinner. You don't want to be in either position.

This lifetime, death may come via lung disease, pneumonia, an asthma attack, or a combination of issues.

✳✳✳

CANCER IN THE EIGHTH HOUSE

Sexual Intimacy

Consider incorporating food into your sex life in some way. That could mean researching different forms of food play or becoming an expert at preparing delicious aphrodisiacs for your lover. Those with Cancer in the eighth house prefer slow, gentle lovemaking that includes lots of stroking, kissing, and petting. They enjoy breast and nipple stimulation immensely.

You crave genuine intimacy, and that can only be accomplished by maintaining balance. Don't focus so much on your lovers' emotional needs that you neglect your own. Likewise, make sure you're really ready to have sex before you make any plans to do it. You shouldn't do it just because your lovers think you're really nice or you feel sorry for them.

Your Elevated Self-Image

Familiarize yourself with the concept of ancestral memory as it relates to traumatic events (especially the maternal line). Consider how you may have inherited pain and sorrow from your parents, grandparents, or great-grandparents that might manifest as negative beliefs and behavior patterns in your life today. You will feel relieved, refreshed, and empowered by doing the work.

Chances are that you are already aware of the negative traits of influential women in your life, but you may not be aware of how deeply affected you are by it. While the effects of negativity are almost always apparent, the cause is not as easy to understand. It is suggested that you take note of the disempowering beliefs that led the women in your family to make the choices they made. Make it a point not to perpetuate dysfunction. Resist the urge to use emotional blackmail to get others to do what you want.

Your Secret Power

People with Cancer in the eighth house can become excellent mediums and are able to more easily enter transcendent states during deep meditation.

Transformations and Endings

Eighth house Cancerians may avoid change in order to avoid hurting other people's feelings. They're the types to remain in unhappy relationships or circumstances in the hopes that things will change eventually. It's fine to show others compassion, but don't forget to show yourself some by nipping things in the bud when necessary. The biggest thing you can do to grow spirituality and facilitate change is make peace with the past. Accept that whatever happened cannot be changed, learn from it, and do your absolute best to move on with your life.

People with this placement may pass away this lifetime from a disease or affliction inherited from your maternal line.

★★★

LEO IN THE EIGHTH HOUSE

Sexual Intimacy

If you want to enjoy a satisfying sex life, it is critical that your partner makes you the center of attention and spoils you rotten! Candlelight dinners, soft music, the works. . . . People with Leo in the eighth house want to be treated with all the pomp and circumstance of royalty by their significant others. They require a lot of attention and are extremely high maintenance in general. They should never date anyone who is not willing to cater to their ego, or who equally likes to be the center of attention, which could trigger competitive or resentful feelings.

Foreplay is probably more important to you than you know. Once you find a lover who genuinely enjoys the pre-show just as much as coitus, you will have amazing sex.

Some eighth house Leos may start a row with their partner just for the hell of it. They may want to see how their lover reacts under pressure or simply as a source of titillation. They don't even understand why they do it.

People with this placement may be too overprotective of their partners, but they mean well. Unfortunately, sometimes their concern may be interpreted as bossy or domineering. Men may feel emasculated by their eighth house lioness.

Never cheat on someone with Leo in their eighth house; they never forgive disloyalty.

Your Elevated Self-Image

It's okay if you want to be in the spotlight. Just make sure the purpose is to serve and enlighten others, not self-aggrandizement.

Eighth house Leos would gain a tremendous sense of pride by producing something tangible that will survive even after their death. Perhaps they should donate a park bench where people will always see their names or create fine art. They don't want to be forgotten, and it will give them peace of mind to know that they will be remembered.

Your Secret Power

Eighth house Leos make talented astrologers and charismatic gurus who may attract many followers.

Transformations and Endings

Unlike those with other signs in their eighth house, Leos manage life's changes well.

Eighth house Leos live in perpetual fear of their egos being crushed. This is probably why they may feel especially vulnerable around people with authority or who are more affluent or popular than they are. They may feel better if they have some sort of platform that they control, where they can freely say whatever they want. This will empower people with this placement and change their lives for the better. If they work jobs where their voices aren't heard, this is an absolute necessity.

Death comes this lifetime as a result of heart trouble, cardiac arrest, or an affliction inherited from the paternal line.

★★★

VIRGO IN THE EIGHTH HOUSE

Sexual Intimacy

Some eighth house Virgos may have grown up in a prudish home, possibly resulting in guilt about enjoying anything but vanilla sex. However, people with this placement will enjoy unconventional sex, but they may prefer to be submissive. Consider voyeuristic play with your lover every now and then. Watch a soft-core porno together or request that you watch each other pleasure yourselves. It will drive you wild! Purchase sexy lingerie or nightwear for your lover as often as you can or feel comfortable doing so—being in control of the little details will turn you on immensely.

Your Elevated Self Image

Those with Virgo in their eighth house would grow if they could learn to get out of their heads more often and become more grounded in their physical bodies.

Many people with this placement hate making mistakes and feel genuinely devastated when other people find out that they screwed up. Sometimes they want to avoid being humiliated after being outed as a human being, so they do stupid things to cover it up. They would grow spiritually if they learned to just admit when something is their fault and take responsibility right away. It's going to sting at first, but eventually it will get easier and you'll find yourself much less stressed out.

Your Secret Power

The creation or use of music as medicine or for the purpose of stimulating transcendent experiences will bring powerful, life-altering results. Embark on research into how music has been used throughout history for these purposes and you will find something valuable.

Unwavering loyalty to whatever you believe in or commit to will attract blessings and happiness, so choose people and ideologies wisely.

Transformations and Endings

Eighth house Virgos require a lot of time to process change. They have to consider every detail imaginable before they feel truly comfortable making a move. However, they will benefit from experimenting with unconventional ideas and hobbies in order to expand their horizons.

People with Virgo in their eighth house may have lost many loved ones to illness and may become paranoid about their health. In extreme cases, they may become hypochondriacs. Ironically, it is their constant worrying that wreaks the most havoc. If they become mindful not to allow their anxieties to get out of control, their lives would be truly transformed.

In this lifetime, death may come from viral illness or intestinal problems. The transition will be quiet or in quiet surroundings.

★★★

LIBRA IN THE EIGHTH HOUSE

Sexual Intimacy

Sexual intimacy is inseparable from mental connectivity for eighth house Librans. Sapiosexuality is common for people with this placement.

Those with Libra in the eighth house require a lot of flirtation and compliments from their partners—even if they've been with them for thirty years. Sex won't be enjoyable for them unless they are certain that their partner finds them physically attractive. It is important, too, that they choose a partner who is more interested in beautiful, passionate sexual experiences versus messy, aggressive sex or unconventional fetishes. To avoid losing the spark in the relationship, seek someone who is comfortable both giving and receiving pleasure.

Eighth house Librans are romantics at heart who burn with desire if they are really into whomever they're dating. However, they can be territorial, possessive, and obsessive. They also may be hesitant to let down their guard for fear of becoming emotionally dependent. Give them time.

People with this placement see beauty where others see imperfection, which makes them quite charming to the opposite sex.

Your Elevated Self-Image

When people with Libra in the eighth house fully comprehend the value of harmonious cooperation with others as opposed to treating engagement and interaction as a means to some sort of end, growth occurs. Learn to genuinely appreciate the beauty and complexity of others.

Those with this placement may have issues with allowing others to get close to them out of fear of being manipulated. Put more trust in the universe that you will be safe.

Eighth house Librans may have a bad habit of making fun of people whom they consider weak, especially if they exhibit their vulnerability in a dramatic way for all to see. People with this placement often find such behavior distasteful, but they should not forget that they are also emotionally vulnerable. The more diplomatic and compassionate they become about such matters, the more they will grow, get along better with others, and feel better about themselves.

Your Secret Power

Blessings and wealth are found through collaborative projects with others. Kindness to all sentient beings, especially animals, will bring blessings. Consider volunteering at an animal shelter, feeding hungry creatures, including people, whom you encounter, or committing to other actions.

Study the philosophy of the arts that you are interested in. For example, flower arranging, tea ceremonies, certain forms of dance, calligraphy, and so forth have a spiritual component to them. You will grow spiritually from the pursuit of a practice that incorporates your aesthetic taste.

Those with Libra in their eighth house are able to communicate with deceased family and loved ones with greater ease than others. Their fascination with death and the afterlife in general makes them more willing to try.

Transformation and Endings

Eighth house Librans should choose their long-term romantic partners with caution, because they tend to transform by taking on other's characteristics more than those with different placements. People with this placement must also learn to choose what they need over what they want more often. It's an exercise in self-discipline that will facilitate other positive changes in their lives.

Those with Libra in their eighth house need to be sure not to forget the importance of self-care, despite the fact that even the most challenging life events will be easier for them to manage than most.

Endings of all kinds will be way less painful if you take a sweet, tactful, diplomatic approach. When you must leave any situation, try your best to neutralize any unpleasant feelings.

Death this lifetime may happen as a result of overindulgence in sweets or of natural causes during sleep. The transition is peaceful and pleasant.

✶✶✶

SCORPIO IN THE EIGHTH HOUSE

Sexual Intimacy

You would do best to choose a partner who would be comfortable exploring the kinky, dark, or unconventional sex that appeals to you. Eighth house Scorpios may enjoy scratching, biting, spanking, or using restraints in the bedroom. You're too intense to attempt to convert someone into a "freak" who isn't naturally so inclined. Don't do it.

Choose a partner who isn't looking for emotional intimacy to happen shortly after sex with you. It will give you the space you need to reflect on what you want without the pressure to make a decision prematurely.

Try not to settle for a partner whose spirit doesn't turn you on. You want to dissolve in a sea of passion and you know it, so don't waste your or someone else's time. The hottest sex people with Scorpio in their eighth house could ever have is with someone with whom they have spiritual connection and who is completely devoted to them.

Your Elevated Self-Image

When eighth house Scorpios become empowered in their own right, their desire to control or manipulate others is significantly diminished. Consideration of the nature of power and how it is best utilized will result in tremendous spiritual and emotional growth.

Many people with this placement have several phobias or are overly suspicious of people they don't know to the point of paranoia. They will grow once they decide to face what they fear and learn to be a bit more trusting.

Your Secret Power

You have the ability to survive the most troubling or challenging situations. The last person standing after an apocalypse would most likely be an eighth house Scorpio.

Dark magic and the mastery of mind-control techniques would come naturally to you, with tremendous success. You would also work well within a coven or other secret society.

You have the ability to bring peace and comfort to the dead and dying. Consider volunteering to clean up cemeteries or working with the terminally ill. Spiritual growth and insight are guaranteed as a result of such work.

Transformations and Endings

Whether you know it or not, you are capable of enduring great transformation and integrating different aspects of your personality into your life, à la Bruce Wayne and Batman. People with this placement are often greatly changed after experiencing traumatic events. They are experts at making lemonade out of the sourest lemons.

Eighth house Scorpios may have abandonment issues that can cause them to be possessive or controlling.

For this lifetime, death could be the result of a sexual assault or another form of violence. The cause of death may be deemed undetermined or kept secret.

★★★

SAGITTARIUS IN THE EIGHTH HOUSE

Sexual Intimacy

Eighth house Sagittarians would be happier with partners who are comfortable with their sexuality and open minded when it comes to trying different things. The approach to sex for people with this placement is playful and fun. Generally, they don't want the atmosphere to be too serious or intense, so it's probably not a good idea to attempt any domination play without having a discussion with them first. People with Sagittarius in their eighth house like to be free, and things could go horribly wrong.

Consider the possibility that your soul mate may be from a different race, ethnicity, or nationality. Don't be afraid to date outside of your comfort zone.

It's important for people with this placement to have complete transparency in their relationships. Being open and honest is everything to them, and until they feel that has been accomplished, they will never commit. People with Sagittarius in the eighth house want their partners to believe in them, and they want to believe in their partners.

Your Elevated Self-Image

Those with Sagittarius in their eighth house do better and feel better about everything when they feel like they have a clear mission or purpose in life. Find your inexhaustible well of faith—you have one, and you can always go to it when life gets you down.

One word of warning to people with this placement: be careful not to become pedantic.

Your Secret Power

You are gifted in your ability to teach and guide others spiritually. Gurus are often eighth house Sagittarians, and you have this potential.

Transformations and Endings

You embrace change with a positive attitude! Feel free to switch gears whenever you feel it's necessary.

Eighth house Sagittarians transform by exploring the spiritual lives and passions of others. Consider engaging in philosophical or metaphysical discussions, writing a blog, or starting a podcast discussing these subjects with others.

People with this placement often endure a series of toxic or totally incompatible relationships before they find the person who is right for them.

For this lifetime, death could be the result of a freak accident, a rare disease, exhaustion, or overexertion.

***

CAPRICORN IN THE EIGHTH HOUSE

Sexual Intimacy

Many eighth house Capricorns immensely enjoy some form of bondage or domination. It's not uncommon for them to enjoy being in control in the bedroom. Find a discreet lover whom you feel safe with to explore possibilities. People with this placement are focused, devoted, and passionate.

It would be wise for those with Capricorn in the eighth house to break up with people they're dating if they prove to be flaky or unreliable. You like to be organized and appreciate people who keep their word, so ignoring red flags will only end in frustration and an inevitable separation anyway.

Your Elevated Self-Image

Reflect on the legacy you would like to leave behind and work consistently to create the life you want.

Your Secret Power

People with Capricorn in the eighth house are much more comfortable with the dark side than most—their own darker tendencies and the darker parts of the supernatural and the world. They are also extremely talented when it comes to creating rituals and initiation procedures.

Transformations and Endings

Transformation comes when eighth house Capricorns learn that their pessimistic attitude is not about "being realistic" but is actually a way to protect themselves against disappointment. It's okay to be practical, but that's totally different from making a career out of being a complainer and a total downer to the people around you.

Those with Capricorn in the eighth house would grow exponentially by carefully reflecting on how their actions contribute to things when they go wrong. They need to work to take responsibility for their part in events even if it is uncomfortable, and resist the urge to blame others exclusively for their problems.

✳✳✳

AQUARIUS IN THE EIGHTH HOUSE

Sexual Intimacy

People with this placement are often commitment-phobes who may feel that long-term monogamous relationships are inherently oppressive by nature. These eighth house Aquarians would be wise to choose a partner who doesn't require them to have a conventional relationship; a jealous, clingy, or possessive lover will make you feel restricted and prevent true intimacy, so avoid these types.

Eighth house Aquarians prize their freedom, their space, their voice, and their right to have desires that have nothing to do with their partners. This may be a source of irritation for their lovers, and they may have been the cause of more than a few heartbreaks. It is advised that those with Aquarius in the eighth house date people who are patient, aloof, or just as distracted as they are to prevent unnecessary drama.

Consider integrating sex toys, web cams, and other technology into your repertoire and watch the sparks fly!

Your Elevated Self-Image

Don't be so hard on yourself and others. It's fine to have high expectations, but make sure they're realistic. Those with this placement need to be careful to avoid group think and maintain their individuality, especially if they are a member of a spiritual or religious group.

Dark, gloomy, or morbid subject matter isn't eighth house Aquarians' cup of tea at all—but what they don't know is that they could offer a fresh perspective on these topics. If they would stop being so quick to dismiss or ignore anything that makes them uncomfortable, they would be surprised at what they learn and discover about themselves.

Your Secret Power

You should consider creating or designing ritual tools and objects with your unique designs, such as sigils and mandalas. Aquarians are visionaries who always have the future in mind. Therefore, the tried and true methods that other signs rely on may not work as well for them. Their power is in their innovation and being unafraid to chart their own course.

Transformations and Endings

People with Aquarius in the eighth house are experts at managing change. They roll with the punches with so much finesse that it often shocks and amazes others.

Eighth house Aquarians will grow exponentially once they realize that their fear of being controlled by others is not about the fact that they like to dance to the beat of their own drum, but is the result of a fragile identity. Once they really internalize the truth—that other people are not a threat or a corruptive influence unless we permit them to be—then they'll be able to relax and give us mere mortals a chance. Stop running. In this same vein, you need to work on allowing other people to grow and change, without making them feel bad about it. You wouldn't want to be mistreated for being you, either.

People with this placement are often obsessed with blaming the government for their hardships and are the chief distributor of the latest trending conspiracy theories.

Some eighth house Aquarians often rely on drugs, alcohol, or time-consuming hobbies with people who think exactly like them in order to avoid people whom they consider less enlightened, or to cope with boredom.

✦✦✦

PISCES IN THE EIGHTH HOUSE

Sexual Intimacy

Be transparent with yourself and your partner about your need for a deep emotional connection. The highest level of sexual intimacy is not possible for you without it. Sex is more of an emotional exercise than physical for you, so think about what kind of person you are seeking. It would save eighth house Pisceans a lot of time and energy if they refuse to accept crude, faithless, inconsiderate, immoral, tone deaf, or materialistic potential partners from the beginning. They are way too sensitive and their ideals are way too lofty to be able to deal with people they consider cold, callous, or uncouth.

People with this placement prefer sexual encounters that may be best described as sweet and innocent. Pastel lingerie, eye gazing, sensuous foot massages, cuddling, taking a bubble bath together, and forehead kisses would bring them great pleasure. If done all at once during the same evening, they will daydream about such a sexual encounter for months. On the other end of the spectrum, consider incorporating water into your lovemaking periodically for mind-blowing sex. The shower, tub, or sex on the beach or near another body of water would be perfect.

It's suggested that those with Pisces in the eighth house only date people who have the stomach to tolerate their idealism and their need to periodically isolate themselves without accusing them of deception, indifference, or neglect.

People that date eighth house Pisces will find them authentic, loving, generous people who don't mind lavishing the object of their attention with lovey notes and gifts. If partners on the receiving end are naturally suspicious of people's motives, they might accuse them of trying to buy their love. Nothing could be further from the truth.

Your Elevated Self-Image

The eighth house Piscean would find travel for the purpose of self-discovery both exciting and liberating. It wouldn't have to be as drastic as relocating to another country or even leaving the country for years (though this isn't a bad idea for them). People with this placement could reap the benefits just by renting an RV and taking to the road for a few months. The insights they receive as a result of such a journey would be deep, penetrating, and inspirational to others.

Learn how to incorporate your desire for spiritual elevation into practical life by figuring out a tangible plan to make your dreams a reality instead of daydreaming about the possibilities.

Your Secret Power

You may already have had encounters with spirits, as you are a natural medium.

Study sex magic, tantric sex, or sacred sexuality. You have the ability to transcend spiritually by learning about and using these methods.

Transformations and Endings

It's important for you to wrap up loose ends when it's time to move on. All too often, people with this placement just move on without officially bringing the last chapter to a close. Make sure you are ending things—relationships, work situations—on the right note.

Eighth house Pisceans welcome change as long as they can determine the spiritual necessity of the changes being implemented. Once they do, they are willing to make the sacrifice without much complaint.

People with this placement often have "Peter Pan syndrome" and are chastised by others for their perceived refusal to grow up. Sometimes the criticism they receive is completely valid, but eighth house Pisceans tend to ignore it for fear that they will lose their fun, childlike nature. They will grow spiritually once they realize that they don't have to sacrifice what makes them beautiful and unique in order to be responsible adults.

Eighth house Pisceans detest asking others for assistance, even if they desperately need it. They don't like the idea of being controlled by other people, so they feel disempowered whenever they feel indebted to anyone else. Actually, the worst thing anyone could say to them is "How could you do this to me after everything I've done for you?" because it validates all of their fears. Their lives will change forever once they realize that there are actually people in this world who genuinely want to help, without a hidden agenda. Seek out and contemplate spiritual teachings that address how to heal from paranoia and mistrust of others.

The Signs in the Twelfth House

*Unspoken Expectations, Confinement,
Karma, Loss, and Self-Sabotage*

THE TWELFTH HOUSE IS RULED by Pisces and Jupiter. This house influences how we handle sacrifice in many forms: personal sacrifice in the service of others, letting go of things (people, material goods) in order to grow spiritually. Our signs in the twelfth house tell us about what desires we might be suppressing or hiding because we are afraid both of how they may be received by others and also that, once we express them, we run the risk of failing in our attempts to achieve them.

✷✷✷

ARIES IN THE TWELFTH HOUSE

Sorrow and Sacrifice

There is a tendency for people with this placement to go above and beyond to inspire, fight, and do favors for others, but there is a danger of burnout and becoming resentful. This can lead to blaming other people for "not having their shit together," instead of reflecting on your motivations for pushing yourself to the breaking point. Is it really about being a good person and helping others, or is it more about fill-ing a void? If your calling to assist others is authentic, then understand that self-care is absolutely necessary in order to do that job effectively. You will grow spiritually by not only serving others but by learning what makes you tick and establishing boundaries. Stop trying to be a martyr. And stop punishing yourself whenever you have a selfish thought or desire.

The twelfth house Aries takes the opinions of others to heart, so any criticism that is deemed unfair or too harsh causes great sorrow and anger. It will serve you better to reflect and try taking things with a grain of salt.

Twelfth house Aries must feel like their lives serve a greater pur-pose or they may experience inexplicable feelings of sadness or confu-sion. They would be much happier if they identify what it is that they want to fight for and devise a clear plan of action.

It's imperative for people with this placement not to repeat mis-takes because they can't control their emotions. Once you see some-thing isn't right, ditch it—or there will be tremendous sorrow in the long run.

Hidden Dreams and Desires

Those with Aries in the twelfth house may dream of providing spiri-tual leadership for their community. They would be exciting, charis-matic guides who explain and emphasize the connection between the microcosm and the macrocosm.

Sometimes twelfth house Aries tend to hide their ambition out of fear of seeming too aggressive, especially if they're women. Perhaps in the past they were taught not to express their emotions or to do so only according to someone else's standards of propriety. Resist any voices that tell you not to exhibit your passions or how strong you are and go after what you want without apology. Consider adopting a hobby or pastime that will help you get more comfortable with your inner warrior, like a competitive sport or martial arts.

You want a partner who will acknowledge and not be threatened by your sexual prowess, even if you suppress it.

Your Past Life

Twelfth house Aries were warriors in their past life. It doesn't necessarily mean that you were Joan of Arc or Shaka Zulu (though you could have been!), but it does mean that you were an aggressive, dominant personality who didn't take any crap and stood up for whatever you believed in.

The end of your life was violent and possibly painful. With this placement and your likely past-life role, it could also indicate death that occurred during the prime of one's life. As a result of this experience, it is absolutely necessary that you enjoy life and never take it for granted, because somewhere inside you know that it can end at any moment.

★★★

TAURUS IN THE TWELFTH HOUSE

Sorrow and Sacrifice

Some twelfth house Taureans give until it hurts. It's great to be a kind, caring person, but if you are always sacrificing what you need and are constantly losing opportunities in order to help others, that's a problem. If this describes you, analyze why you feel that your suffering is less important than the suffering of others. Compassion begins at home.

Those with Taurus in the twelfth house are always haunted by a feeling that they never have enough. This person could have millions of dollars in the bank but still not feel financially secure. Some also tend to have elitist and classist attitudes as well that may make them look down on themselves or others for not having "made it." They need to learn that every human being has value regardless of how much is in their bank account or what they possess. People with shopping addictions often have this placement. Be aware. Check to make sure you're not purchasing self-worth.

Much sorrow from your life comes from being resistant to sudden changes. Learn to accept the fact that no matter how meticulously we plan or "know" something is going to work out, sometimes it doesn't. You'll be so much happier once you become less stuck in your ways and can be more flexible when you have to go left instead of right.

Because twelfth house Taureans hate change, they may continue to forgive people whom they should have cut off years ago, just because they're familiar. It may be difficult, but getting rid of dead weight and toxic people is a worthy sacrifice.

Hidden Dreams and Desires

People with Taurus in the twelfth house may not know it, but deep down inside they long for true love. They would like to know what it feels like to be intensely in love, but they may also fear that level of intimacy.

Your Past Life

In your past life, it is a highly probable that you came from a family that was either extremely wealthy or destitute. Either extreme is what has caused your present fixation on money. You were most likely a business man or woman who lived a very financially secure, comfortable life.

✦✦✦

GEMINI IN THE TWELFTH HOUSE
Sorrow and Sacrifice

People with Gemini in their twelfth house have great ideas that they are willing to share to help others. However, they may find that others benefit more from their ideas than they do, and this may make them resentful. It's important that they consider this possibility before giving away their genius so cavalierly. When considering the consequences of sharing their ideas pro bono, it is equally important that they consider their motivation for doing so.

These people must also consider why others are more successful at implementing their ideas. The most likely reason is that other people actually finish what they start and go the distance instead of being so easily distracted. Procrastination and letting opportunities slip by is how twelfth house Geminis lose the most.

You have a tendency to hide your intellect and analytical abilities from other people, which often may cause them to underestimate you. Though your shyness about exhibiting how smart you actually are caused the issue in the first place, you may place the blame on others for their inability to see what you refuse to show.

Try not to be so fearful about admitting it when you don't know something. No one knows everything, and this is how we learn. You won't lose anything by saying you don't know something. Likewise, don't be afraid to speak up if you are thinking outside of the box. It's okay to consider, implement, and share new or controversial ideas.

Hidden Dreams and Desires

You desire more attention than you realize or are willing to admit to others. Instead of just facing that fact, twelfth house Geminis often become jealous of those getting the kind of attention they would like to receive. As a result, they become duplicitous and malicious, spreading rumors or participating in unflattering gossip. This is a shame because, unbeknownst to them, people tend to listen and believe the words of those with Gemini in their twelfth house. So not only can things get out of hand as a result of their gossiping, it's a waste of influence that could be used to spread and give credence to a more productive message.

Your Past Life

Twelfth house Geminis were most likely writers or the village story-teller in a past life. They would have been a person known for their extroversion, wit, and gift of gab.

Depending on other placements in your chart, there is a chance that either you were involved with ruining someone's reputation as a result of something you said or your reputation was ruined by someone else's words. In either case, this lifetime is about learning the power of communication.

✳✳✳

CANCER IN THE TWELFTH HOUSE

Sorrow and Sacrifice

People with Cancer in the twelfth house carefully guard their emotions because they feel vulnerable. As a rather high-maintenance person emotionally, it doesn't take much for these people to feel unappreciated, offended, or ignored. They must learn that brooding over real or imagined slights is counterproductive and a complete waste of precious time and energy. People with this placement must also learn to put themselves in other people's shoes a lot more than they do. It would be helpful for them to stop and ask themselves how someone else feels or may interpret the situation.

Twelfth house Cancers must learn that sometimes it's okay not to be perceived as the carefree nurturer who's always smiling. If you are upset with someone about something they did that really bothers you, please don't just brush it off and keep it to yourself. Stop prioritizing the feelings of others over your own all the time or there will be cause for great sorrow in the long run.

Be careful of becoming too clingy. There is a danger with this placement of being oblivious to healthy emotional boundaries, and this could eventually result in losing your most beloved. Stop being annoying. Give people space and a chance to miss you now and then. It's good for everyone involved.

Beware not to use drugs, alcohol, or food as ways to cope with sorrow or disappointment.

Hidden Dreams and Desires

Whether they're aware of it or not, twelfth house Cancerians are terrified that others will discover how emotionally vulnerable they really are. They hide behind a mask of cordiality, but their secret desire is to tell the world how they really feel.

Your Past Life

Those whose twelfth house contains the sign of Cancer were most likely midwives, wet nurses, gynecologists, or some other profession related to the care of women or nurturing others.

Many twelfth house Cancerians inherit intense or extremely emotionally traumatic family histories that they have to resolve.

✳✳✳

LEO IN THE TWELFTH HOUSE

Sorrow and Sacrifice

Those with Leo in the twelfth house are compassionate people who don't mind being the power behind the throne. They enjoy providing others with the love and support they need, but may tend to overdo it and end up sacrificing too much in the end. They may not mind, though, if the mission is greater than them and is a worthy cause. Spiritual growth occurs when they don't seek attention for its own sake or at all but simply focus on the task at hand.

Twelfth house Leos tend to take themselves way too seriously and may be seen as a bit of a "buzz kill" to others. They mean well when they encourage others to get back down to business, but they need to be aware of coming off as bossy or annoying.

Those with this placement tend to downplay their creativity because they enjoy being perceived as responsible. This is a shame because they actually would enjoy exploring their creativity if they took it more seriously. These are the types who often mock others for majoring in the arts or becoming freelancers.

This placement may produce people who become obsessed with maintaining their reputations to the point that they are willing to do almost anything to save face. This could result in making very poor decisions in a desperate attempt to remain in control, which can result in unimaginable loss or sorrow if they go too far.

When someone brings an issue they have with you to your attention, try to listen instead of expecting your ego to be stroked just the way you like it. You may not appreciate the delivery, but that doesn't mean that there isn't truth to what is being said. Avoid unnecessary power struggles.

Hidden Dreams and Desires

Twelfth house Leos idealize being humble, but they secretly dream about being the ones to call the shots. This hidden desire may cause them to dislike others who may be seen as prideful or unabashed about their ambition. Many deal with these feelings in a healthy way by becoming the power behind the throne. That way, you will have the control you crave but you won't have to be the face of the product or message. Instead of hating the peacocks, learn to acknowledge their usefulness.

Your Past Life

Twelfth house Leos were most likely aristocrats, royalty, or a member of some sort of privileged caste or class in the societies they lived in. You were envied and admired, which could be the reason why a part of you still craves this kind of attention but is also repulsed by it as well.

Depending on other factors in their chart, some twelfth house Leos may have risen to the top at the expense of others. This may be another reason why they are focused on serving others this time around.

★★★

VIRGO IN THE TWELFTH HOUSE

Sorrow and Sacrifice

People with Virgo in the twelfth house are extremely sensitive to the feelings and criticisms of others and may jump through hoops to please them. While it's great to be accepting of input from others, it's not okay to completely forfeit your autonomy over your own life. These types of people will cancel the fun plans they had in advance to help someone who approaches them with a sudden minor issue that can totally wait until they return. This is unacceptable. A balance must be found between your desire to assist others and taking care of yourself; be careful not to make the former your top priority, because it doesn't work.

People with this placement experience sorrow and loss as a result of being too set in their ways. They would benefit from doing something unpredictable once in a while, which will have the same effect on their lives as opening up a window in a stuffy room.

Twelfth house Virgos let people get away with trying to be slick or glossing over their mistakes because they want to avoid confrontation. Then they complain that people think they're stupid or are trying to use them. They need to learn that it's okay to pull people's cards and let them know you're paying attention to the details even if you don't seem to be.

Hidden Dreams and Desires

Those with Virgo in the twelfth house often keep their criticisms and judgment under wraps, but they dream of counseling or guiding others on best practices, especially as it relates to health, fitness, or spirituality.

Your Past Life

Twelfth house Virgos were most likely doctors or healers in their past lives. They may have also been indentured servants or enslaved. What is known for certain is that these people were bound to serve others, whether they liked it or not.

★★★

LIBRA IN THE TWELFTH HOUSE

Sorrow and Sacrifice

People with Libra in the twelfth house are emotionally tender and vulnerable. It can be very difficult for them not to put their all into their relationships, which can sometimes lead to them feeling drained or exploited if their efforts are not reciprocated. Twelfth house Librans may sometimes tolerate repeated disappointment in relationships out of a sense of loyalty. They need to stop ignoring the toxicity because they would rather focus on when things are going right instead of wrong. This coping mechanism will eventually wreak havoc on their concept of self-worth and cause great sorrow. If there are more bad times than good or if you're constantly in pain in any relationship . . . let it go.

Rather than establish clear boundaries and expectations in relationships to protect themselves, twelfth house Librans would rather shift the blame onto other people. They are often the victim of deception, which makes their failure to guard themselves all the more baffling. However, twelfth house Librans are magnets for liars and narcissists, and they tend to be oblivious to the fact that this may include their closest friends or family members. As a result, they are often shocked when they're betrayed. Get your head out of the sand and open your eyes. If someone's behavior seems curious, shady, or sketchy, it probably is—even if it's your husband, your friend of thirty years, or your mom. Sorry.

Twelfth house Librans may sometimes tolerate repeated disappointment in relationships out of a sense of loyalty. They need to stop ignoring the toxicity because they would rather focus on when things are going right instead of wrong. This coping mechanism will eventually wreak havoc on the person's concept of self-worth and cause great sorrow. If there are more bad times than good or if you're constantly in pain in any relationship . . . let it go.

While you are better at working independently than with others, you should work on becoming more open to collaborating. You will miss opportunities if you don't, and finding out later what you could have accomplished will bring sorrow.

People with shopping addictions often have this placement. It's important to be aware of when you really want or need something versus being bored or purchasing things as a way to compensate for difficult emotions.

Hidden Dreams and Desires

More than anything else, deep down inside twelfth house Librans desire a soulmate or a twin-flame connection. They are way more emotionally dependent on the people in their lives than they would ever feel comfortable admitting, which may make them deny that this is what would make them happy. Not because they don't believe in love, but because they may perceive themselves as introverted, loners, or too weird to ever find such a connection.

Your Past Life

Twelfth house Librans were most likely artists or some kind of creative people in their past lives. Whatever their work entailed, beauty was the focal point.

Sometimes people with this placement experienced great pain or loss as a result of a failed relationship (platonic or otherwise). Selfishness or greed was most likely the issue.

✳✳✳

SCORPIO IN THE TWELFTH HOUSE

Sorrow and Sacrifice

People with Scorpio in the twelfth house are usually the hidden mystics among us who have no idea of their abilities. People usually feel their power even if they're not exactly sure what they're feeling or why they're feeling it from you. As a result, people may want to borrow your things, not realizing that they're actually trying to comprehend your psychic imprint. Thus, it's no surprise that twelfth house Scorpios don't often see anything they lend to others ever again unless they harass someone for their stuff back.

Twelfth house Scorpios need to beware the tendency to confuse sex with intimacy. People with this placement can also be prone to melancholia or depressing thoughts. If you see yourself going in that direction, try and change the energy by doing something that makes you happy or "changing the channel" to a program that won't take you there.

Those who have Scorpio in their twelfth house will grow spiritually by keeping in mind the unity and divinity of all things, especially themselves.

Hidden Dreams and Desires

Twelfth house Scorpios have a clear moral compass, and this can lead them to repress their deep desire to explore their power and sexuality. It's easier to hide, fear, minimize, or deny their attraction to things that may be perceived as dark or taboo rather than compromise their beliefs. They will grow spiritually once they accept life in totality, and that there is nothing wrong with going off the beaten path or at least learning about the ideas of the people who travel that way with a more open mind.

Your Past Life

Twelfth house Scorpios were probably scientists, investigators, or inquisitors in a past life. No matter what the actual profession was, it required critical, analytical thinking skills and an obsession with getting the job done.

People with this placement could have been the type of people who were willing to do anything to get what they wanted. That could take the form of manipulation, witchcraft, sexual favors, theft, or murder.

✦✦✦

SAGITTARIUS IN THE TWELFTH HOUSE

Sorrow and Sacrifice

People with Sagittarius in the twelfth house must examine their beliefs to prevent them from feeling lost or like they're not living up to their standards. They would do well to be open to more diverse experiences and people in order for them to grow on the soul level. They should never sacrifice more than they have to give, or their lives may begin to feel composed of one burden-filled day after the next, which will lead to grave unhappiness.

Twelfth house Sagittarians have strong convictions and a hidden optimism or naiveté that may not be apparent to others or themselves. That's why it's easy for them to become victims of con artists. This is especially true if the charlatan convincingly appears to be a shining example of what someone in their religious or spiritual community is supposed to be.

This placement often causes people to doubt their ability to guide others, because they don't believe that they're worthy or knowledgeable enough. They usually are, but they sacrifice opportunities for expansion because they are constantly focused on their perceived limitations and imagined inadequacies.

Hidden Dreams and Desires

The twelfth house Sagittarian genuinely wants to believe in themselves and wants others to know that their success is a product of their grind and nothing else. However, they should learn not to feel ashamed of their belief in divine guidance. Deep down inside they believe in God, the power of ancestors, spiritual guides, and guardian angels and feel connected to something much bigger than themselves, even if they try to hide this fact from others. Once they stop feeling ashamed or hesitant about admitting such feelings, they will be more flexible and more relatable to others.

Your Past Life

Twelfth house Sagittarians were most likely explorers, teachers, or philosophers in their past life. Regardless of their actual occupation, they were free spirits who insisted on living life on their own terms even if they were forced by circumstances to only do so in private.

Depending on other aspects, such people may have hurt others in their past life as a result of their devil-may-care attitude. While most people would agree that being yourself is the best way to live, the reality is no one is an island. Twelfth house Sagittarians may have been free, but may have caused their loved ones embarrassment or great pain while they were living their best lives.

✱✱✱

CAPRICORN IN THE TWELFTH HOUSE

Sorrow and Sacrifice

People with the twelfth house occupied by Capricorn are usually deeply insecure but are never quite sure why they don't feel like they're good enough. Even when things are going their way, they may struggle with that nagging feeling that they are still stuck. This will be a lifelong battle, but continuing to challenge Saturn's bullying instead of conceding defeat will empower them. A remedy for these people is to live as righteously as possible. That will be their most potent weapon against Saturn's oppressively high standards. People with this placement are notorious for being too hard on themselves. Just because things don't work out as planned sometimes doesn't mean that you're a failure or less deserving of happiness. Self-flagellation isn't the key.

People with this placement like to project an avant-garde or edgy image, but they would actually achieve more if they followed convention more than they do. It's not that they can't be eclectic, but they would experience less sorrow or loss if they travelled the beaten path more often. Make your peace with regular people and try to find a way to incorporate the best of both worlds.

Twelfth house Capricorns may resist changing their repertoire and may have a fear of success. Change is necessary sometimes. Get out of your own way!

Hidden Dreams and Desires

Recognition for their abilities and freedom from toil is what twelfth house Capricorns desire most. They also long to be recognized for their innovative ideas, and they get more discouraged than they admit to being when they are not constantly validated and applauded.

Your Past Life

Twelfth house Capricorns were either politicians or tough-as-nails business people in their past lives. They were most likely highly efficient and, depending on other factors in the chart, possibly ruthless in the pursuit of their goals.

In a past life, those with Capricorn in the twelfth house may have died with the burden of knowing that their actions caused the untimely death or suffering of other people.

✳✳✳

AQUARIUS IN THE TWELFTH HOUSE

Sorrow and Sacrifice

People with Aquarius in the twelfth house are interested in universal laws, cosmology, and the inner lives of others. You think a lot about matters related to the collective consciousness and you're always sensitive to the needs of groups, so you love to help. However, with this placement there is a very real danger of overly identifying with the community to the extent that your individuality may get lost.

Twelfth house Aquarians may hide how avant-garde, unconventional, or weird they are for fear of being unaccepted in or even exiled from their communities. These people are so used to being the eccentric outcastes that, when they do find people who accept them, they are so relieved and grateful that they may go above and beyond for them. This is not necessary. Remain true to yourself.

There is a danger of making poor choices as a result of peer pressure (regardless of how old you are) and the desire to be on-trend.

Hidden Dreams and Desires

More than anything else, twelfth house Aquarians desire to be free. They want to be liberated from the constant pressure to compromise who they are or how they express themselves just to get along with others. Since life often demands this, life itself seems to be an oppressive chore sometimes. They would do best to accept themselves and seek comfort in spirituality of some sort in order to cope.

Your Past Life

Twelfth house Aquarians were most likely rebels or eccentric people and may have been considered outcasts in their societies. They stood out in the crowd, for good or for bad.

People with this placement may have been careless or impatient, which caused their deaths.

✳✳✳

PISCES IN THE TWELFTH HOUSE

Sorrow and Sacrifice

People with Pisces in the twelfth house tend to hide their caring and compassionate nature for fear that it will get in the way of getting things done. They are usually way more sensitive than they admit to being, too, which means they tend to hide the fact that they're hurt, offended, or displeased. That's not good, because that may lead to holding a grudge against people who might not realize and who would apologize if they knew. This can lead to the premature ending of relationships that could have been fulfilling and long lasting had the Pisceans just been upfront about their feelings. Their intuition probably tells them not to distance themselves after these situations occur, but one of their biggest life lessons is learning to trust their gut instincts.

Twelfth house Pisceans must be careful not to become addicted to things or people.

People with this placement are often squeamish about expressing their beliefs or trusting their intuition. As a result, people may not know or understand their boundaries, and this may result in unnecessary sorrow, loss, or conflict.

Hidden Dreams and Desires

More than anything else, twelfth house Pisceans want to fortify the connections they have with close friends and family, whether they know it or not. If they do some serious self-reflection, they will see that this is the case, but they might not know how to accomplish it. The secret is figuring out a way to become more comfortable exhibiting their truly caring nature without feeling like a chump for doing so. Perhaps they could consider putting together an annual barbecue or creating gift baskets for those they care about.

Your Past Life

Twelfth house Pisceans were probably poets, clergy, or shamans in their past lives. Regardless of what their actual title was, their jobs required unlimited compassion and care for other people.

Sometimes people with this placement were emotionally damaged or mentally impaired people. They could have been cognitively or developmentally disabled, or had trouble with alcohol. Death could have occurred as a result of their condition.

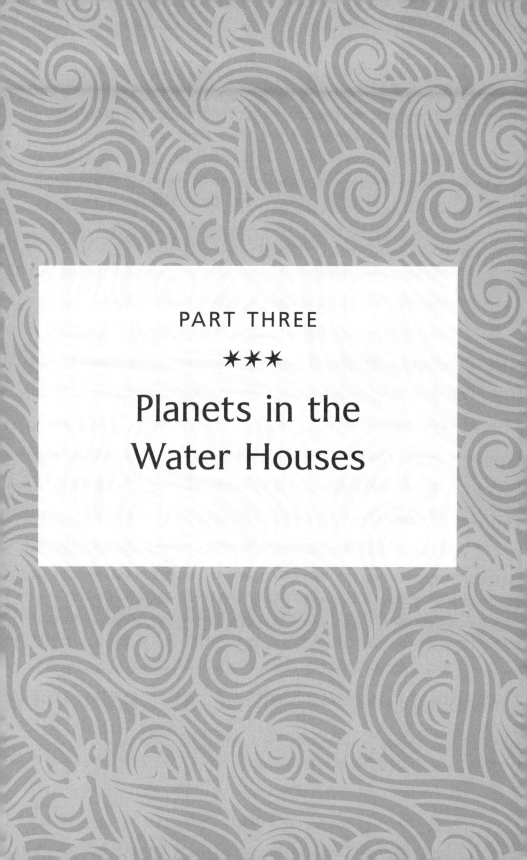

PART THREE

★★★

Planets in the Water Houses

The Significance of the Planets in Astrology

AS WE ALL KNOW, THE PLANETS in our solar system each have different characteristics in terms of atmosphere, topography, or appearance. In astrology, they are symbolic reflections of the different aspects of our personality. Ten main astral bodies are analyzed in Western astrology: the sun, the moon, Mercury, Venus, Mars, Jupiter, Saturn, Uranus, Neptune, and Pluto. Astrologers observe the placement of these astral bodies in a person's chart based on where they were positioned in the sky at the time of birth. Then they interpret the archetypical qualities associated with each and how they may negatively or positively affect the individual. The ten astral bodies are always moving at various rates of speed so some planets remain in a particular sign for shorter or longer lengths of time.

Every zodiac sign is ruled by a certain planet or planets; this is also known as the planet's domicile. Similarly, some modern astrologers also recognize each house as being ruled by a certain planet or planets. More traditionally, the relationship between houses and ruling planets is determined solely by where they fall on the individual's birth chart. You will see this reflected in the water triad analysis samples in the conclusion, where the fourth, eighth, and twelfth houses are ruled by different planets in the different individuals' charts, creating relationships between the planets and the houses unique to that individual. This is also true of the signs: in any individual's birth chart the signs may, and often will, be associated with different planets than their ruling planets.

Ancient astrologers attributed certain characteristics to the planets they observed. When a sign is said to be ruled by a particular planet it means that sign contains the energy of its "parent." For example, if your sun sign is Pisces then the ruling planet is Jupiter. That means that Pisces is informed by Jupiter's expansive, idealistic, and dreamy qualities. So the parent planet has its own traits, as does the "child" astrological sign. In the early days of astrology there were only seven celestial bodies acknowledged. They knew nothing about Neptune, Pluto, and other planets and stars that were discovered after there was technology to see them. Even today Vedic astrologers do not acknowledge these other bodies, as they consider them not important enough to mention. Western astrologers have adapted a co-ruler system to acknowledge the old ways and incorporate new discoveries, so you will see that some of the houses have more than one ruling planet.

There are four primary categories of astral bodies that are analyzed in a horoscope: luminaries, personal planets, social planets, and transpersonal planets. The sun and moon are luminaries and along with Mercury, Venus, and Mars comprise what are known as the "personal planets." The personal planets represent our basic motivations and urges as human beings. We may come from diverse backgrounds but we all basically have the same fundamental needs and desires. However, individuals have different approaches or outlooks on life that determine how they feel about and pursue these needs and desires. Jupiter and Saturn are the two "social planets." Social planets represent how we interact with other people. Uranus, Neptune, and Pluto are called the "transpersonal planets," aka the "modern planets." Unlike the personal or social astral bodies that focus on individuals, these planets affect generations because they move much more slowly. It's important to make the distinction between how astrology enthusiasts calculate and define a generation versus how social scientists calculate and define them. Astrology determines a generation by the sign Pluto is in. For example, baby boomers equate to Pluto in Virgo, Generation X equates to Pluto in Leo, etc.

Personal Planets

The Sun (Ruler of Leo)

The sun, like the moon, is a luminary and not a planet. Luminaries give us our primary sources of light during the day or evening. Likewise, they are considered the most important astral bodies in astrology because they highlight the primary expression of who we are.

Almost everyone on Earth knows the constellation the sun was in at the time of their birth because of the popularity of horoscopes in various print media for almost a century; knowing your sun sign became a part of pop culture. However, most people will be totally baffled if you ask them what, for example, their moon or Mercury signs are, because in their minds the sun sign is "theirs" and the other astral bodies are rarely, if ever, discussed in this context. The interesting thing about that is that there are a lot of people out there who have never identified with their sun sign and have no clue as to why, because information regarding the other personal planets hasn't gone mainstream yet. So if you don't identify with your sun sign it's probably because your moon sign or some other planet has modified the expression of your sun sign in a profound way.

The sun represents how we shine. In other words, it shows us the image in our minds of our ideal self and how we want to express that to others. It also represents our ego, willpower, and integrity. The sun transits into a different zodiac sign every month.

The Moon (Ruler of Cancer)

The moon reflects our emotional nature. It reveals what makes us feel safe, what comforts us, what nourishes us, and how we nurture others. It represents the subconscious mind, instincts, habits, emotions, sense of self-preservation, and moods. When we refer to our "gut reaction" to situations and circumstances, we are talking about our moon sign. The moon transits into a different zodiac sign every two to three days.

Mercury (Ruler of Gemini and Virgo)

Mercury symbolizes how we communicate, our intelligence, and how we process information. Mercury transits into a different zodiac sign every three to four weeks.

Venus (Ruler of Taurus and Libra)

Venus represents how we express love, how we relate to love, what we find attractive, and what we enjoy. It also indicates our social style and what we're looking for in a relationship. Venus transits into a different zodiac sign every four to five weeks.

Mars (Ruler of Aries and Co-Ruler of Scorpio)

Mars symbolizes how we express our anger and sexuality and desires, how competitive we are, and how bold we are. It also represents how we argue and what we're willing to do and how far we're willing to go when it's time to take action. Mars transits into a different zodiac sign every six to seven weeks.

Social Planets

Jupiter (Ruler of Sagittarius and Co-Ruler of Pisces)

Jupiter symbolizes what inspires us to grow, what we have to teach, how lucky we are, our religious or spiritual inclinations, and how optimistic we are. It also indicates how adventurous we are and our level of interest in education. Jupiter transits into a different zodiac sign every twelve to thirteen months.

Saturn (Ruler of Capricorn and Co-Ruler of Aquarius)

Saturn represents our endurance, how we perceive boundaries, limitations, and setbacks, and how mature or disciplined we are. It also symbolizes our ambition, our desire for security, how well we conform with established norms, and our ability to function as productive members of our societies. Saturn transits into a different zodiac sign every two to three years.

Transpersonal Planets

Neptune (Co-Ruler of Pisces)

The Neptune sign in an astrology chart reflects the dreams of an entire generation. It symbolizes a collective vision of an ideal world. The house placement of Neptune in an individual's chart will indicate how that person will aid in the construction of that world. Neptune transits into a different zodiac sign every fourteen years.

Pluto (Co-Ruler of Scorpio)

The Pluto sign in an astrology chart reflects the key challenges of an entire generation. It reflects people's dark side, how they define power, and what they need to purge as a collective consciousness. Pluto transits into a different zodiac sign every eleven to thirty-six years.

Uranus (Co-Ruler of Aquarius)

The Uranus sign in an astrology chart reflects how a generation expresses its uniqueness and how its members are impacted by new technology, rebellion, or social upheaval. Every generation witnesses changes in the world and the Uranus sign reveals how people feel about and cope with those changes. Uranus transits into a different zodiac sign approximately every eighty-four years.

The Planets in the Fourth House

Home, Family Influence, Safety, and the Self

***

THE SUN IN THE FOURTH HOUSE

Those with the sun in the fourth house seek approval from their families before making major life decisions. However, they must be careful not to miss auspicious opportunities while they wait for an endorsement.

People with this placement are usually extremely close to their mothers and see them as role models. This person's mother may have had a playful, artistic temperament and may have seemed more like a big sister to her children than an authority figure.

Sun in the fourth house people are more on the introverted side, but they enjoy discussing their family, especially if the discussion relates to ancestral traditions, genealogy, or history. People with this placement are very much interested in their ancestral heritage and seek to incorporate that wisdom into their daily lives in some meaningful way.

People with the sun in the fourth house can be either traumatized or validated by how others perceive them. It is important for them to accept and love themselves, regardless of the cheers or boos that may come their way.

It's important for these people not to romanticize the past. Whether it be the world one hundred years ago or their parents' lives, they need to remember that people are people. There's nothing wrong with celebrating noteworthy achievements and admiration, but keep things in perspective and don't ignore flaws. Be here in this time, now.

Reflect on what you need to feel protected and safe.

Those with the sun in the fourth house are usually chill, laid-back people outside the home, but they prefer to rule the roost. Their home is their castle; they will defend their right to invite anyone they deem worthy, and they will not hesitate to ask someone who is misbehaving to leave. People with this placement exhibit great pride in their home and enjoy lavishing snacks and attention on their guests. They appreciate guests who applaud their interior design skills and the delicious refreshments they serve. Complimenting them will guarantee an invitation to their next soirée.

Fourth house suns are reliable, loyal people with pleasant dispositions. Even so, just like with houseguests, this placement makes people discerning about who they allow into their circle of trust because they value privacy and discretion. If these people tell you their business, they must really like and trust you.

If you must buy a gift for someone with the sun in their fourth house, make sure you give it a lot of thought. They appreciate a more personal touch.

People with the sun in the fourth house are ready, willing, and able to offer useful advice.

★★★

THE MOON IN THE FOURTH HOUSE

The moon in the fourth house indicates that one has a close relationship with one's family, especially the mother or maternal figure. In fact, people whose mom is also their best friend probably have the moon in the fourth house.

You may have more of a spiritual affinity toward the culture, traditions, or spirituality of the maternal line, and this should be honored in some meaningful way. Overall, though, you will feel that your cultural heritage and traditions should be respected and observed. When they are not, you may feel extremely guilty.

There is a tendency to be controlling or overly demanding to family members in an effort to keep everyone together, but it can backfire and actually push them away. Balance is key, so be mindful of this propensity. Likewise, people with this placement take commitments seriously and expect others to do the same, especially when those commitments pertain to familial responsibilities.

The home must be a place of peace and tranquility or the person with the moon in the fourth house may become depressed and despairing. Keep moving until you find the perfect home for you, no matter how long it takes. Your emotional health is highly dependent upon your happiness at home.

People with this placement experience extreme homesickness whenever they travel far from home. They are the least likely to move far from their home base and may prefer to live in the same place for their entire lives. This placement would even be happiest working from home. People with the moon in the fourth house tend to become more attached to their homeland as they get older. Expats with this placement tend to return home even if they've lived abroad for a significant amount of time.

Fourth house moons love to cook and feed other people. They may also enjoy housework and can't relate to those who dislike domestic chores.

People with the moon in the fourth house would find it therapeutic to live near the water or have a view of it. If this is not possible, then collect seashells and colorful or interesting rocks found near or in the water. It will bring you pleasure and peace.

They may tend to obsess over being safe and secure. They should take whatever precautions necessary but avoid becoming obsessed and taking things too far.

People with this placement tend to cling to the past so tightly that they are constantly reminiscing and trying to recreate happy moments from the past. They might even still have the same hairdo or haircut they had during their heyday. Everyone gets nostalgic now and then, but these people need to connect to the here and now more in order to grow.

If these people upbringing was unsettled or traumatic, they may be insecure and require a lot of reassurance from their partners. Likewise, when under stress, people with this placement may regress to coping behaviors they engaged in as a child.

Discretion is important to the person with the moon in the fourth house. Once a confidence is betrayed, it will be difficult for them to heal from it.

These people have a powerful imagination that is prone to exaggeration. This increases the likelihood of drama, and may facilitate misunderstandings of what others try to communicate to them. The result is insomnia, overeating, and explosive emotional outbursts. Meditation or yoga may help with this.

You may be easily influenced by those closest to you, making you feel extreme pressure to submit to their will over your own. Don't lose sight of your priorities. If there are people who make you feel guilty for wanting to be your own person and asserting your independence, you must put an end to it. There's nothing wrong with giving your loved ones an ear, but when it gets to the point where you're being infantilized then it's about something else. Think about it.

✦✦✦

MERCURY IN THE FOURTH HOUSE

Clear, consistent communication is key to maintaining healthy relationships with your family.

Education, reading, writing, and learning were encouraged while growing up. Continue to pursue these as an adult to feel fulfilled. Fourth house Mercurians usually had mothers who encouraged them to seek knowledge and who stressed the importance of critical thinking. As children, they were allowed to dream and perceive as they wished, and they shared their active imaginations with the adults around them.

People with this placement love to research their family histories and treasure old photos and letters and enjoy hearing what family members who have passed on used to say or think. What they learned at home is much more influential than what they learn from outsiders. These are the people who are always quoting their mothers. If you hear "Mama used to say . . ." on a frequent basis, the speaker may have Mercury in the fourth house.

People with this placement feel safe and secure at home. They may want to consider working from home, if possible; this would make them very happy. It brings great joy for the fourth house Mercurian to have a home library or a quiet place to study. You'd be best served by maintaining an atmosphere of peace and harmony in your home.

People with Mercury in the fourth house usually enjoy the intellectual stimulation at school but they would benefit most from smaller learning environments where teachers can give them a lot of one-on-one attention.

Children are often fond of people with Mercury in the fourth house and they, in turn, enjoy teaching kids cool, interesting facts.

The best way to get on the bad side of someone with this placement is to embarrass them publicly or expose a secret they trusted you with. They will never get over it, even if they say they have. It's also not a good idea to lie to people with this placement. They are great at remembering details; they're the type of people who crack cold cases by recalling a teeny-tiny but critical piece of information that finally leads to the capture of the perpetrator.

Fourth house Mercurians tend to accumulate a lot of emotional clutter. It may be a good idea to journal or find some other way to get all of those feelings out, instead of trying to manage them all internally. Try writing poetry.

These people love to learn and are great at recalling information, but spiritual breakthroughs come when they get in tune with how they genuinely feel about things rather than rely on a prix-fixe menu of responses or beliefs that they have been taught.

If you were bullied or mocked as a child, spend some time reflecting on how this may have affected you and take the necessary steps to heal those scars.

When people are feeling down and are seeking a few kind words, they usually call on fourth house Mercurians, who never disappoint in that department.

★★★

VENUS IN THE FOURTH HOUSE

Fourth house Venusians often have a wonderful relationship with their mother or whoever acted as a maternal figure to them growing up.

People with this placement either grew up in beautiful homes that other people envied or they had a lot of beautiful things. If this was not the case, then they dreamt about it often. No matter where you live or how small your living space is, you should make your surroundings as aesthetically appealing as possible. This will uplift you. Purchase the most beautiful, comfortable home furnishings and décor you can afford. Don't overlook the little details and don't forget the fresh flowers or plants. You will feel happier surrounded by lovely things.

Consider hosting business associates or influencers that you'd like in your corner for a soirée or two at your home. Make sure whatever you serve them is beautifully presented, with good music and delicious cocktails. It's more than likely that you'll get whatever you're seeking from them.

You would be happier and boost your confidence if you shared your creativity with others on a consistent basis. If your day job doesn't involve creating or making things to share, then consider choosing a hobby that would allow you to do so.

People with Venus in the fourth house are super loyal and are the type of people who stand by their partner even if they no longer look good or become severely disabled. However, women with Venus in the fourth house may attract more than their share of narcissists or men with mommy issues. They would be wise to take note of this and decide early on whether or not they want to put up with it, because once they emotionally invest they are less likely to do anything about it or make any changes.

People with this placement must live with people who allow them to safely express their emotions or they will suffer tremendously. They shouldn't be the only ones comforting and being supportive of others and must guard against giving too much without receiving.

✦✦✦

MARS IN THE FOURTH HOUSE

Your family encouraged you to be yourself, but that doesn't mean people should be expected to accept unruly behavior, long-winded rants, or dramatic emotional outbursts. Check yourself and try to be objective about your behavior. You may find it necessary to leave your birthplace or family environment if you cannot reconcile your differences.

People with this placement are usually fiercely independent and prefer to be the head of their household even if they aren't footing the bill. In that vein, if fourth house Martians are being financially supported by others or are crashing on someone's couch, they are most likely unhappy about it. Rather than stew over this inconvenience, it would be better for them to contribute more by taking on more of the cooking or household chores. Even if it's not your turn to do it, your pride will be eased a little.

Be careful with open flames in your home as this placement is prone to house fires. Don't leave candles unattended or fall asleep smoking.

People with Mars in the fourth house would benefit from spending more time outdoors for their overall wellness. If they have an office job, the weekends should be spent being active outside of the house.

They may have witnessed power struggles between the adults at home growing up. They need to be wary of recreating that drama in their own domestic situation. Transformation for this placement happens once they commit themselves to unlearning any toxic behavioral patterns and messages they learned during childhood. Instead of seeing oneself as a victim, they would do better to consider themselves survivors.

Though these people may be a bit shy around strangers or when placed in unfamiliar situations, they are more extroverted when they are around people and in environments they're comfortable with. They might be prone to showing off if they've had a few cocktails. People with Mars in the fourth house are usually ready and willing to do favors for their friends with little or no hesitation.

Fourth house Martians insist on knowing where they stand with people they care for. It's not because they're being pushy, it's because they genuinely want to know. If they like someone romantically and they're ready to take things to the next level but the other person isn't, that's a serious problem for them. The best thing for them to do in that situation is give that person a date by which they need to express their desire for deeper intimacy and a commitment, and if they don't, then move on. Don't try to badger, argue, or manipulate your way into a more serious relationship, because even if you get what you want now, you'll be humiliated when you are reminded that this is what *you* pushed for even though you knew your significant other wasn't ready.

They must learn that the way other people do things is not always wrong and that their way is not always better. Everyone is not going to respond to stimuli the same way, and that's okay.

These are the type of people who do well saving face in public if they get upset. However, as soon as they get home; their composure is out the window and there will be a confrontation. If the situation involved the disrespect of a loved one, then all hell will break loose— they are extremely protective of those they care about.

A word of warning is to make sure you follow up on anything you initiate. There is a tendency for people with this placement to be gung-ho in the beginning of an endeavor but then lose steam. Don't leave people hanging.

✳✳✳

JUPITER IN THE FOURTH HOUSE

People with this placement usually have a close-knit family who enjoys spending time together and have a nice home. Their childhood was happy and surrounded by attentive, loving adults who spoiled them rotten. They would benefit from remaining in their place of birth, or in proximity to it.

Invite people you care about to your home for no reason other than to spend time with them. It doesn't have to be a big fancy dinner; just keep in touch offline and in person as often as possible. You will feel more secure and happy.

Follow your moral convictions, especially as they pertain to family and domestic matters.

As much as you value the past, be careful not to obsess over it or risk trying to constantly recreate it. You may have warm memories, but try not to get stuck.

Not being permitted to freely express oneself during childhood may result in some people with this placement feeling like they don't want to be parents. Reflect carefully on this, because you may just need to heal from the trauma of suppression.

Fourth house Jupiters are intellectually curious and were most likely some of the smartest kids in school.

Spiritual guides and ancestors are always close by and ready to communicate. In addition, people with this placement have powerful gut instincts that rarely fail them. They probably have an amazing tale to tell either about the time they trusted their intuition and it saved them from disaster or the time they failed to heed their internal alarm system.

Jupiter in the fourth house usually creates conventionally

professional types even if they don't see themselves that way in the present. If an opportunity presents itself, don't automatically reject it, even if it doesn't seem like "your thing"—wealth may be on the horizon!

These people are always rewarded for their generosity, so they should never hesitate to lend a helping hand for fear of permanent loss. Helping others attracts blessings.

✶✶✶

SATURN IN THE FOURTH HOUSE

People with this placement may have had a cold parental figure or serious responsibilities at a young age. This may mean that they are not comfortable unless they are working or excessively burdened in some way, often because they were only considered useful as a child when they were doing chores. To heal from this, reevaluate your source of confidence. You don't have to carry loads like a Georgia mule to matter!

Sometimes those with Saturn in the fourth house may have parents who cared about them but who, for whatever reason, didn't know how to appropriately express their love in a nondestructive way. They may have been forced to grow up fast and had their childhood cut short because they had strict, cold, neglectful, or cruel parents who insisted that they "learn the truth" and told them about the "realities" of the world. These children were often not permitted to dream or spend one minute in "la la" land, or to believe in imaginary friends or figures like Santa Claus or the tooth fairy. They might have been latchkey kids as well, or the emotional distance from their family made them feel desperately alone. As a result of a difficult childhood, fourth house Saturns are resilient and unflappable.

People with Saturn in the fourth house may struggle with figuring out who they really are and what they actually want as a result of the restrictive, controlling, or punitive nature of their upbringing. The adults around them may have tried to break their spirit by telling them they would fail if they didn't do exactly as they were told or live the way they were expected to live. This may haunt them and make them hesitant to follow their dreams or pursue an "unauthorized" path.

Break the chain by showing your children the warmth, kindness, and compassion you wish you had received from your own parental figures. If your birth family is gone or you don't speak anymore, your friends often become your family, and these relationships can be healing.

It may be therapeutic to confront the adults who tried to crush you or who brought you misery growing up. You will feel so much better getting it out in the open and out of your system! If you possess family heirlooms or antiques, think about what energy comes with those objects. What memories do they conjure for you? Consider whether it is healthy for you to keep them. Forgive yourself for the mistakes you've made so you don't carry the additional burden of regret. Let go.

Those with Saturn in the fourth house may dislike change; for some, it is even like Kryptonite is to Superman! They get a sense of peace from predictable routines and are genuinely upset when they have to switch it up. That can be fine, but don't wait until the roof caves in and you're forced to make a move. Learn to be more flexible.

✱✱✱

URANUS IN THE FOURTH HOUSE

This placement is often indicative of an unusual childhood and even more unusual relatives, or it could mean that the person with Uranus in the fourth house themselves will build and become such a family once they settle down.

The mother may have been eccentric, encouraging an unconventional parent-child relationship that might have seemed strange, unacceptable, or inappropriate to others. She may not have had the emotional maturity or desire to express her love the way society expected her to; she wasn't "into the whole mommy thing." This may have embarrassed or scarred the children deeply as they longed for a more traditional situation. They may also have been separated from their birth family via a traumatic situation such as the constant relocation of a parent, adoption, foster care, or the pursuit of political asylum.

As they grew up, there was never a dull moment in the house; there was constant stimuli or emotional turmoil. They also may have been sickly or misbehaved a lot during their childhood and spent a considerable amount of time in and out of hospitals, rehab, asylums, or juvenile hall.

These people are perceived to be weird by other people because they do everything their own way, so their routines, habits, and perspective on things will be way different than the norm.

Someone with Uranus in the fourth house enjoys nurturing others, so long as that role doesn't require them to sacrifice their peace.

✱✱✱

NEPTUNE IN THE FOURTH HOUSE

People with this placement often had parents or caregivers that were aloof, depressed, intellectually challenged, or medicated or intoxicated most of the time. They might have spent most of their childhood caring for the parents rather than the other way around. Despite that, they become quite defensive if other people talk negatively about their family.

Your family may have been considered eccentric in comparison to those around you, and this may have affected your self-image. In addition, people with Neptune in the fourth house tend to have families that infantilize them, regardless of their age or experience.

People with this placement may have had childhood experiences that are unfathomable or baffling to other people and themselves. Usually, they don't realize just how different their upbringings were to others' until they get old enough to share and compare their experiences.

This placement may make people confused about who they are or cause them to suffer from anxiety because their parents projected their self-image and long-lost dreams onto them. It is recommended that they focus on their spirituality to help them heal from the unrealistic expectations placed on them and the pressure to be someone they were not. This shouldn't be a problem since these people are already spiritual people even if they haven't formally declared a position or joined a group.

If your family is broken up or estranged from one another, it would be a good idea to reflect on how this has affected you and to seek help to heal the emotional scars. Sometimes people with Neptune in the fourth house were scarred after a family secret was exposed. This might have destroyed an illusion, which caused them to rethink everything. Don't hesitate to abandon morals and values that were reinforced by your family but no longer resonate with you as true or necessary.

People with this placement usually feel a deep spiritual connection with their ancestors or cultural legacy. They exhibit pride in their racial or ethnic background. Be careful, though, not to transfer negative feelings onto your cultural heritage as a whole if you don't get along with your parents.

If you have children, be conscious of the tendency for those with Neptune in the fourth house to use emotional blackmail to get their kids to do what they want. Resist this urge at all costs; it may irreparably damage your relationship.

"Home" is wherever there is warmth, support, and acceptance, not necessarily a place made out of brick and mortar. People with this placement often feel that the entire universe is their home. The more stressful their childhoods were, the stronger this belief will be.

Fourth house Neptunes feel most comfortable when their artistic interests are an integral part of their domestic lives. They would really enjoy starting an art collection, and they are probably the neighbor that is always blasting their favorite music.

People with Neptune in the fourth house almost always attract friends with mental-health or substance-abuse issues. These people must not be permitted to drain you of critical financial or emotional resources just because you have a history together. Don't lose your shirt or deal with unacceptable or dangerous circumstances just because you were in the same class in fifth grade. Avoid allowing them to stay with you, no matter how close you are. Things are almost guaranteed to get ugly after a while and you'll regret it!

Fourth house Neptunes may develop a savior or martyr complex. In addition, people with this placement may be partial to lying or embellishing a story to get what they want. They can be very manipulative. Watch out for this tendency.

You have a spiritual, almost telepathic ability to communicate with family members whom you consider close. Those with Neptune in the fourth house are intuitive overall, and may often receive divine messages from spiritual guides, angels, or ancestors. If they are so inclined, they should hone this skill.

✦✦✦

PLUTO IN THE FOURTH HOUSE

People with Pluto in the fourth house most likely had a very dark childhood. They may have witnessed or experienced abuse, bullying, betrayal, depression, or drug addiction; there might be a family history of violence or sexual molestation or rape by relatives. If that is the case, then the victims were probably expected to remain quiet and not report these incidents or discuss them with anyone. Perhaps they were even threatened with physical harm or with being cut off from the family if they ever chose to seek justice or share their pain with outsiders.

In some cases, people with Pluto in the fourth house may have been removed from their abusive homes or completely abandoned by their mother. If the latter, they may have serious abandonment issues and seek constant reassurance from the people around them that they will never leave.

If you grew up amid a traumatic situation or abusive family or with a parent with anger issues, it would be wise to reflect on how that behavior may have affected the way you relate to others. As a result of the emotional trauma that those with this placement often experience, people with Pluto in the fourth house may feel immense shame about their childhood. Their grudges may make them doubt that anyone can be trusted, and they may refuse to start a family of their own for fear they'll scar someone else as badly as they have been scarred. It's time to end the cycle by acknowledging what happened without rationalizing or denying anything. They should strongly consider seeking professional help. The biggest mistakes they can make are to minimize the challenges they endured as a child or recreate the same environment they were raised in.

There is a high probability that you have frustrated, angered, or alienated your family by believing or living very differently than the way you were raised. If you have never had a calm, rational discussion addressing the tension, you might initiate one; if it doesn't work then consider keeping your distance, because things can take a sudden nasty turn.

People with this placement may have gotten the shock of their lives when someone close to them died or moved away unexpectedly, leaving a terrible scar on their heart that will take a lifetime to heal.

Resist the urge to become a dictator at home. Just because you pay the bills doesn't give you the right to be abusive to others. If you feel it does, then perhaps you should make arrangements to live alone.

Withstand the need to rely on anyone else to empower, validate, or nurture you. If you do receive it from others, that's great! But never forget that it's still your own responsibility, first and foremost.

The Planets in the Eighth House

Talents and Skills, Relationships,
and the Occult

✳✳✳

THE SUN IN THE EIGHTH HOUSE

Actively seek out profound experiences that the average person wouldn't dream of. It will make life seem more exciting and make you feel more alive. Those with the sun in the eighth house are usually very comfortable discussing or participating in activities that other people cower at the mere mention of. This is a source of great pride for them, but they should be careful not to allow others to exploit their bravery or their desire to be noticed by daring them to do stupid, irresponsible things. Use your courage to fight for something worthwhile; you have this ability in order to help you get things done, not for the amusement of individuals who don't even have a quarter of your guts.

If you're interested in the occult or mysticism, don't hesitate to pursue those interests, but be sure not to focus too much on the superficial aspects. Don't lose sight of the ultimate goal, which is self-improvement and spiritual growth.

Eighth house suns may develop a reputation as rather goth or strange because they don't hesitate to discuss dark, overtly sexual, or other taboo subject matter. While this may be amusing to them, it would be wise for them to consider how such candor may affect their reputation or long-term goals should an influencer or colleague become disturbed. These people may get involved in weird or fringe subcultures simply as a way to get the attention they secretly crave or to prove a point. They often don't realize until much later that that was what it was all about the whole time.

People with the sun in the eighth house may take their desire for power to a dark place. They may become so obsessed with being in control that they are willing to do anything. It's important for them to consider the feelings of others or the potentially dire consequences of their pursuit if things don't go according to plan.

People with this placement may have suffered the death of their father before they were born or at a younger age, or he may have abandoned the family altogether.

Most people form their self-image based on interpersonal relationships and the perceptions of others to a certain extent, but this is especially true for this placement. Don't forget to check in once in a while to determine if you really agree with these assessments of your character that have been placed upon you by others, rather than blindly accepting them. It's important for eighth house suns not to permit their own personal experiences to be trivialized for the sake of belonging. If other people in the group feel a particular way about something but your experience of that something is different, resist the urge to try to shoehorn their perspective or deny yours.

People with this placement would be wise to live healthy lifestyles and consume heart healthy foods for increased vitality.

People with the sun in their eighth house are not quick to settle with just anyone for a long-term relationship. They would be happiest with someone with a regal or aristocratic quality. This carries over into their sex life. These people have an extremely high libido and sex is one of their favorite pastimes, but they want it to be with someone worthy of their time. If they have sex without any real chemistry between them and their partner, they feel gross.

★★★

THE MOON IN THE EIGHTH HOUSE

People with this placement have extraordinary healing abilities. Consider studying reiki, massage, or some other form of hands-on therapy to help others. It will give you an extra source of income and provide a great sense of personal satisfaction. Counselors, psychics, healers, detectives, and high-level occultists often have this placement.

The moon in this placement can make someone appear mysterious, aloof, or completely detached from reality.

The moon in the eighth house produces strong feelings about all matters related to esotericism, mysticism, death, and other keywords associated with this house. These people may have many strange or unusual occult interests, abilities, or spiritual experiences and may be attracted to religious or occult studies. They aren't very interested in the technical details or whether something can be proven scientifically; logical understanding is unnecessary. It's all about how people and situations make them feel. It's all about soul connections.

People with this placement have a strong sixth sense and can usually spot a con artist or a poser a mile away.

Paranormal experiences are more common for eighth house moons and they may be accused of lying because their reports are so extraordinary. The truth is always stranger than fiction for them. They also contemplate their dark side more than others, and this may make them seem a bit strange or morbid. They aren't afraid to die and don't feel creeped out by discussions related to death, dying, or end-of-life care.

Sometimes this makes them daredevils; not because they have a death wish, but because they genuinely understand the gift of life.

Even so, people with the moon in the eighth house can easily become depressed by their circumstances or the state of the world in general because they are natural empaths. They would be wise to limit their exposure to painful, disturbing, or negative imagery that may trigger gloomy, unpleasant thoughts.

The female lineage of those with the moon in their eighth house has had a major impact on them. For good or for bad, they have been greatly affected by how their mothers treated them. Sometimes they are haunted by the traumas of their maternal ancestors. They would be wise to learn what afflictions, addictions, or situations they endured and identify how this may have affected them on an unconscious or spiritual level via epigenetic memory. These people may also have female ancestors who were very spiritual or active in their religious or spiritual communities as leaders or healers.

It is extremely difficult for eighth house moons to seek help when life gets them down. They want to clam up when they actually should be communicating more—they need to resist this urge! This will be a challenge because they don't like owing anyone anything or having people tell them how they should feel. They are also extremely private and highly discerning about whom they share their deepest feelings and thoughts with. They're the type of people who are absolutely devastated by betrayal of any kind. If they tell friends to keep something a secret, they expect them to keep their word. It goes both ways, too. They feel special when they are told that they are receiving information that had never previously been shared with anyone else. They value the trust and exclusivity, and want to understand what makes someone tick.

This is the placement of a deep, sensual, intense, and loyal person who takes a while to let others in because they know they are super sensitive. There is a tendency to become extremely emotionally attached and dependent on loved ones. They tend to take on the characteristics of their romantic partners, and have a strong desire to please them. They are prone to becoming clingy and when relationships go south or a breakup occurs it is beyond devastating. They would do well to try to mitigate this. Don't be afraid to love or trust just because sometimes things don't work out. That's life.

This placement can make one obsessed with sex. When they're not doing it, they're usually thinking about doing it. They are in bliss when they meet a partner who is equally sensual, which is rare. People with this placement should not try to participate in hook-up culture because sex and their emotions are indivisible and they can get hurt.

The moon in the eighth house may attract situations and events that are emotionally devastating or just plain odd. They find themselves wondering why they have to endure such chaos, but it actually helps them grow.

✳✳✳

MERCURY IN THE EIGHTH HOUSE

People with Mercury in the eighth house are born investigators who enjoy uncovering taboo facts and shocking secrets and solving mysteries of all kinds. Eighth house Mercurians enjoy decoding and analyzing others. They are experts at seeing through the masks.

They enjoy digging beneath the surface because they want to know what things really mean. They like books and documentaries that present the reader or viewer with secret histories or less well-known facts. They find it amusing when someone is exposed as being fake.

People with this placement are often communicating or researching on behalf of other people. They may be interpreters, translators, or ghost writers. They have probably fixed more resumes and written more papers for others than any other placement. They make great writers and often have a dark sense of humor that not everyone appreciates.

Eighth house Mercurians may like to dominate and impress others with their intellectual ability to the point of being manipulative. Make sure your quick wit and legendary sarcasm don't spawn a horde of hidden enemies.

Though people with this placement may not tell others everything they're thinking, their words have an impact on others when they do. Be careful what you say to others in anger because it is certain to be excessively harsh. It's better to walk away, log off, or return a phone call later after you've calmed down.

This placement produces a person with a dry wit, a lot of sarcasm, and a vicious tongue. You don't want to get told off by these people because they will do their absolute best to obliterate you. People are often shocked when they get into an argument with them and somehow they seem to know what they're most insecure about. Mercury in this position allows them to expertly read between lines their opponent didn't even know they drew.

Eighth house Mercurians may alienate other people by freely discussing dark, controversial, or taboo topics as easily as others discuss the weather. There is also a tendency to criticize others for their spiritual or religious views while not being clear about what they themselves believe.

Someone with Mercury in the eighth house can be trusted with secrets. They are very discreet. But don't try to keep secrets from them because they'll eventually find out whatever it was that was being so desperately hidden.

Choose a long-term romantic partner who doesn't mind discussing their deepest darkest secrets, what makes them tick, and their childhood traumas or major disappointments. Intimacy is established once you're satisfied that you know all there is to know. You'll know instinctively if they're lying about telling everything, and will continue to try to get them to admit that they haven't. Therefore, people who would rather keep the past in the past or who cannot discuss the past because it will get them in trouble with the law shouldn't date someone with Mercury in their eighth house. They will never just let it go, and it might end up with a lawsuit or someone getting busted.

✶✶✶

VENUS IN THE EIGHTH HOUSE

Those with Venus in the eighth house are the kind of people that very few people know very well, if at all. They are akin to the locked door that, once finally opened, reveals yet another door, and so on. They cherish depth and despise shallow people and conversation.

Eighth house Venusians are virtually amoral—they just don't experience things through the lens of right and wrong, moral or immoral—but because of societal pressure to choose between "light and darkness" they may be confused by their indifference until they make their peace with it. These people care about their appearance and are sensitive to criticisms about it. They are often considered attractive even if they aren't conventionally beautiful.

People with Venus in the eighth house are extremely hard to fool as they have a sixth sense about the hidden dynamics between people. They have strong intuitions and are always ready to give useful advice and insights to anyone in need.

These people have a pronounced interest in magic, spiritualism, metaphysics, mysticism, cosmology, and the occult. They enjoy researching and learning about all of these subjects.

Eighth house Venusians are very sensual people who appreciate erotica and all things related to love and romance. At some point in their lives, they may work in environments where these subjects are freely discussed.

However, they tend to be attracted to shy, aloof, or introverted people for long-term relationships. They don't want someone who is capable of connecting with just anyone; they want to be able to unlock the safe themselves. They are intense, passionate people who seek to merge mentally, physically, materially, and spiritually with their partners. Relationships with others are never superficial, as they find anything "surface" impossible at worst and unpalatable at best. If they feel they are more invested than the other person, they will leave.

Eighth house Venusians are not interested in sex until they meet someone they genuinely make a soul connection with. Until they find the right partner, they have no problem being celibate. Hook-ups, one-night stands, or any form of sexual activity without that spark are impossible for them. They live for meaningful, passionate encounters.

Those with this placement don't fear death, the unconventional, or anything taboo. They tend to find the beauty in dark people, imagery, and subject matter. People tend to either love them or hate them; there is rarely a middle ground for those with Venus in their eighth house.

✦✦✦

MARS IN THE EIGHTH HOUSE

Those with Mars in the eighth house will be aggressive and persistent about getting what they want. They may even turn to the "dark side" by seeking to obliterate who or whatever is in the way. It's a very bad idea for people to violate the privacy or cross the boundaries of eighth house Martians. They will get beyond pissed off and retaliate.

When people with this placement decide to delve into the occult, they do it to try to understand how to efficiently use their power and overcome their fears. People with Mars in the eighth house often hide their passion, intensity, and ability and willingness to engage in battle. That side of them is only revealed if they feel they have no choice. Usually, the circumstances that cause them to finally unleash the beast have to do with issues surrounding disrespect or injustice of some kind. They won't just stand on the sideline and watch someone being victimized.

Sometimes these people are exposed to violence or explosive situations that they somehow managed to endure with far less damage to their psyches than other people might suffer. They are the proverbial phoenix that keeps rising from the ashes. Betrayal or traumatic experiences cause these people to be somewhat paranoid and may have triggered the ability to see someone's true colors even when others may be fooled.

Choose long-term partners who would give you the shirt off of their back, just as you would do for them. You won't feel safe or secure if you're more invested than they are. Sex with eighth house Martians is often mind-blowing and exhausting because they can keep going much longer than people with other placements. People with this placement may enjoy rough sex; it would be wise to express this before becoming intimate to avoid frightening or offending their lovers. At worst, failure to mention their tastes may result in litigation.

Freely sharing resources with others will help them stay connected to others and soften them a little.

People with Mars in the eighth house may go from zero to a hundred and back again in the blink of an eye. They expect everyone to just get over it.

✳✳✳

JUPITER IN THE EIGHTH HOUSE

These people are deeply spiritual, with the ability to guide and comfort others who are experiencing a crisis. They might consider volunteering or working at a shelter or a crisis hotline. Donations of all kinds to those in need attract blessings. Strangers often confide in eighth house Jupiters because they are usually kind and open-minded. As a result, they may find that they attract a lot of wounded people and others who seek out their help.

Once those with Jupiter in the eighth house experience a pleasant paranormal phenomenon, get results after casting a spell, or achieve something off of their vision board, they will be thrilled and won't stop trying to make it happen again. People with Jupiter in the eighth house may discover that they are excellent occultists and can manifest the changes they desire without trying that hard. Such individuals will also receive useful insights and advice from occultists and diviners in their service.

Unwavering faith that things will work out for the best after experiencing setbacks and challenges will often yield unexpected good fortune if not outright miracles.

Jupiter in the eighth house gives the person an unusually comfortable attitude toward the dark matters signified by this house. People with this placement are totally at ease exploring dark philosophies and theories regarding death or the afterlife. There is something comforting to them about life one day coming to an end, even if they never express such thoughts to anyone else. They are not afraid to die or what may happen to them after death.

People with Jupiter in the eighth house are highly intelligent and exist in the world quite differently from everyone else. They not only ask deep questions but they also seek out the answers themselves rather than just accepting what authority figures have to say on the subject. Depending on the people around them, that fact alone will make them unconventional or a serious threat. They're determined to do this and will not be persuaded to stop, which may cause them to withdraw from others who may try to make them submit to the opinions of the experts. These people have probably been called "old soul" their entire lives and tend to be quite deep and philosophical. They enjoy discussions that others may consider way too heavy.

Eighth house Jupiters may not be aware of it, but they have the capability to learn foreign languages faster than other people and often become fluent with very little effort. This is especially true if their desire to learn will help them solve a riddle or communicate with people who have the knowledge they're looking for.

Someone with Jupiter in their eighth house would be wise to choose a long-term partner who has compatible religious or spiritual beliefs. Failure to do so may cause unnecessary drama, fights, and/or a nasty breakup. These people tend to have many lovers and are very open sexually. Serial cheaters often have this placement.

Travel to exotic destinations and befriending foreigners will expand your horizons and help you grow spiritually.

✳✳✳

SATURN IN THE EIGHTH HOUSE

People with Saturn in the eighth house may have many quirks, fears, and phobias that can impede their enjoyment of life. Don't just ignore this—seek help if you've already lost people or opportunities because it's gotten out of hand.

Such people may have grown up hearing their parental figures constantly complain about all of their burdens and sorrows and having too many responsibilities in relation to the care of the eighth house Saturns. This affected them deeply and they probably internalized feelings of guilt, which is the source of so much misery for them.

If people with Saturn in the eighth house grew up poor, there is a risk that they will use that experience as a rationalization for running themselves ragged. Ironically, they are way too busy to really enjoy the comfort they work so hard for. It would serve them to take a step back and examine this tendency. You don't have to work all of the time to accomplish your goals. If you find yourself cancelling your plans with loved ones, it may be time to reflect on your own happiness and how others may feel about your constant rejection. You may think you are getting what you want now but not have anyone to share your happiness with later.

Business or financial success may occur in the person's later years.

These individuals detest change, so the sooner they see it coming, the better. Out of all the placements that fear and despise change, this one feels it the strongest. This person is a creature of habit like no other.

Eighth house Saturns may suffer from terrifying nightmares or fear the dark. People with this placement also may feel extreme anxiety when they are the center of attention or when others are being negatively critical of something they worked hard on. These people usually feel like there's never enough time to get things done, which in turn may manifest into a fear of death. They would be a lot happier if they would learn to relax and just do their best. There are probably very few people that die having accomplished everything on their bucket list.

Stop pushing people away. If you need help, there's no shame in asking! People with this placement may lose a relationship with someone they care about deeply because they were too set in their ways. It's highly likely their beloved asked them repeatedly to go with the flow and relax a bit and they refused or weren't able to. Instead, they drove them away with their incessant nitpicking and criticism and dislike of compromise. Often, it's not until later in life or after a rite of passage, like marriage or the birth of a child, that it suddenly hits them . . . the other person was right. If they realize the person that left them or whom they broke up with was actually right for them, they may feel immense sorrow.

Asexuality, frigidity, or a lack of interest in sex should be bluntly discussed with potential partners to avoid an uncomfortable situation or a breakup later.

Unlike most, people with Saturn in the eighth house are aware of their limitations, insecurities, and flaws. They may appear stoic to other people, but they have plenty of feelings; they just don't like exhibiting their vulnerability for all to see.

★★★

URANUS IN THE EIGHTH HOUSE

People with this placement can seem as though they have multiple personalities and may be feared or distrusted for a while until others get to know them better. This is because they have absolutely zero fear of transforming themselves as life demands, and these changes are often drastic and totally unpredictable. They are the types to look "normal" in May, but by June they may be sporting a blue and yellow Mohawk.

Eighth house Uranians are firm believers in other worlds or dimensions, and they feel somehow connected to them or believe they may be the key to their true origin. These people often have the ability to see, sense, or hear ghosts or other spirits, but they usually cannot sustain it for long. They may have precognitive visions of their own death or the demise of others.

They desire to free the world from oppressive rules, values, and routines, and they wouldn't see anything wrong with joining a cult if they agree with the group's mission.

People with Uranus in their eighth house seek out long-term romance with people who are just as weird as they are or who are at least tolerant of their eccentric behavior and lifestyle. For them, intimacy with anyone begins with the acceptance of who they are. This placement indicates these people may have unconventional sexual habits or fetishes, or the places or people that turn them on are very different from what most other people find desirable.

This planet in this house is indicative of quick death with minimal suffering. One minute they're here, and a few seconds later they're gone.

✦✦✦

NEPTUNE IN THE EIGHTH HOUSE

People with Neptune in the eighth house are no strangers to uncanny spiritual experiences and may even consider themselves to be mystics. These people have an interest in aliens, psychic phenomena, ghosts, and astral projection and are intuitive and often fascinated by the occult, especially as it pertains to invoking spirits that dwell in other dimensions.

These people are highly sensitive and often don't know how to cope with their overwhelming feelings and psychic impressions. They can read someone like a book, even if they just met them. Many people with this placement have powerful, predictive dreams and the feeling of déjà vu is a more common occurrence for them as well. Some people with this placement are indifferent about living or dying; it simply doesn't matter to them.

Eighth house Neptunes are secretive about sharing their dreams and deepest desires for fear others will laugh or find them odd. They are in danger of being manipulated and deceived by predators that take advantage of their idealism.

People with this placement are often their own worst enemy. They may traffic in disturbing, self-destructive thoughts or behaviors including contemplating suicide or the use of and possible addiction to drugs or alcohol.

People with Neptune in the eighth house need to realize that everyone can't be and doesn't want to be fixed. You need to avoid the tendency to bring yourself to utter exhaustion in your attempt to save someone from themselves. It's their path; know your limitations before disaster strikes. Likewise, choose long-term partners because you love and respect them rather than because they may give you an opportunity to give them a spiritual makeover.

★★★

PLUTO IN THE EIGHTH HOUSE

People with Pluto in the eighth house are not only comfortable with change but with radical change that no one else sees coming. In fact, they rarely fear death because they already experience so many major transformations and changes in fortune.

Character is developed through traumatic experiences, which are usually handled bravely; people with this placement manage to not only survive emotionally traumatic events, but their lives often end up being better than ever. However, they must use their will to put the forces in motion.

This placement is common for spiritually inclined people of all kinds, especially those with an attraction to darker or esoteric teachings. They are especially attracted to the occult sciences and are good at them. These people grow spiritually via the serious study of these subjects. They are excellent researchers. If the answer exists and they desperately want to know, they'll find it.

Eighth house Plutonians bond with others by seeking to understand them on the soul level. They are deep, penetrating people who may become obsessed with their significant others.

The Planets in the Twelfth House

Past Lives and Nurturing the Self

✱✱✱

THE SUN IN THE TWELFTH HOUSE

People with sun in the twelfth house love to fantasize about being famous, but they are equally terrified by the idea for fear of being emotionally overwhelmed by all of the attention. Hard times tend to take a toll on these people's self-esteem. It would help them if they could understand that everyone experiences failure and disappointment in life, and they don't have to permit life's challenges to destroy them. Cancel the pity party for a change.

Such people may have unusual interests, even to other people who study the occult. They would be best served by using their occult knowledge to petition or summon help during dark times.

People with the sun in the twelfth house were usually prominent in their past lives. As a result, they may get offended more easily by the slightest rejection or have an inexplicable air of entitlement that can sometimes rub people the wrong way. However, it's because of this regal air that they excel when they are allowed to lead the pack and make the rules. Likewise, there is a tendency to resent authority figures and being told what to do.

✱✱✱

THE MOON IN THE TWELFTH HOUSE

People with the moon in the twelfth house can tend to be hypersensitive. They are like psychic sponges, so it is imperative that they decompress at the end of the day. They would benefit immensely from frequent sea salt baths and a lot of peace and quiet, especially after socializing for long periods of time. It's also a good idea for people with this placement to find a way to express their feelings. Journaling, painting, or psychotherapy may provide much needed relief.

Twelfth house moons may be attracted to activism, nursing, or any position that will allow them to empathize and sympathize with those down and out or suffering. These people believe spiritual enlightenment is best expressed through service to the underdog. This placement has a need to nurture others and their compassion seems boundless, but there is a tendency for them to give until it hurts. It's great to help others, but this should be called out for exactly what it is: compulsive and extreme behavior. It's okay to leave something for yourself.

The moon in the twelfth house may cause depression, which can be especially pronounced if the person was emotionally starved or had a lack of security in the home as a child.

Many people with moon in the twelfth house are hiding a terrible secret about themselves or someone close to them. This placement often indicates people who have inherited a lot of family dysfunctional patterns from their ancestors, which can take the form of spiritual, emotional, or physical abuse. There is also a higher probability that the source of the problem was related to alcoholism or drug addiction. Twelfth house moons may have known their mothers in a past life and were born to her in this lifetime to resolve whatever emotional issues affected their prior relationship. People with twelfth house moons may also have been a nurturing maternal or paternal figure for their communities in their past lives.

As mentioned before, twelfth house moons are super sensitive and may experience dramatic changes in their mood, which can make it difficult for them to clearly identify what they need to do to stabilize themselves. It is advisable to study stress-relief methods and centering techniques for their moon sign and incorporate them into their daily lives if possible.

Resist the tendency to hide or deny your emotions. If you're feeling overwhelmed, take a moment to clearly identify what the problem is and exactly what you need to resolve it. If there are other people that have information or resources you can use to speed up the resolution process, then don't hesitate to reach out to them for support.

✳✳✳

MERCURY IN THE TWELFTH HOUSE

Twelfth house Mercurians are exceptionally bright, with the ability to comprehend even the most complex metaphysical and occult subjects, and they are capable of clarifying these topics for others.

Dark, unconstructive, demoralizing thoughts may plague twelfth house Mercurians. When these negative thoughts float to the surface, get in the habit of writing them down and rewriting something positive in their place. Don't let a pessimistic rant last so long that you lose all your steam to get things done. Eliminate known frenemies and don't waste precious energy on online debates or squabbles with random trolls and haters.

In their previous lifetime, people with Mercury in their twelfth house were intelligent and had powerful, active minds. As a result, these people often experience a sense of knowing things without understanding how they know them.

People with this placement are more likely than others to be affected by what their mothers said, heard, or experienced during their pregnancies. If you strongly dislike or distrust any immediate family members, it may be because you remember an unpleasant message that was transmitted to you at that time. If you are willing or able to ask your mother who or what upset her the most during her pregnancy, you may get additional insight.

Resist the urge to remain quiet when you know it would be best to speak out. You have interesting things to say and great ideas that would be of interest to others if you would stop trying to fly under the radar.

There are aspects of your personality that may seem contradictory to you, but they actually aren't. If you start to explore who you are and what makes you tick, you'll be certain to discover how it all comes together.

✦✦✦

VENUS IN THE TWELFTH HOUSE

People with this placement would do well living somewhere in peace and seclusion where they can create and discover the meaning of life in their own time, on their own terms. Venus in the twelfth house people don't require a lot of material possessions to feel wealthy or accomplished in life.

Twelfth house Venusians were most likely admired for their creativity, physical attractiveness, or sense of style during their past lives. They were most likely financially comfortable if not rich. People with this placement were often unabashed hedonists or they managed to meet their soulmate in their last lifetime and lived out their days in a happy, healthy relationship with their partners. No matter how old they were when they passed away, they weren't ready to leave because they genuinely enjoyed their life. Their soul seems to remember all of the fun they had last lifetime, so if things are a bit slower this time around, it's very disappointing. This is especially true if you don't feel you've found your ideal mate.

There is an attraction to emotionally unavailable lovers, which brings immense pain and sorrow—but it's their own fault because they aren't sure what they really want. Twelfth house Venusians must be very careful if they engage in love triangles, infidelity, or "harmless" flirting with someone they know is already involved, because it could lead to big trouble. For this placement, such behavior is a sure sign of low self-esteem. On the other hand, resist the tendency to suppress your passion. If you have feelings for someone, don't be afraid to let them know how you feel. Just try to shift your attention to those who are available to you.

If you were raised around adults who engaged in unhealthy relationships, then you may have internalized inappropriate responses or bad behavior from your elders. In order to minimize the odds that you will duplicate the folly of the people you witnessed, it's suggested that you be clear about what you want. Spent some time visualizing how you want your life and love to be.

✱✱✱

MARS IN THE TWELFTH HOUSE

Resist the urge to suppress anger or rage. Tell people when they have annoyed or displeased you rather than just hope that they'll figure it out. Don't allow yourself to be silenced for the convenience of others.

People with this placement have very strong principles and strong opinions regarding the nature of society in relation to human suffering.

Twelfth house Martians may have had soul-crushing childhoods where the adults were negative, power mad, intimidating, and over-bearing. As a result, they may tend to avoid conflict and often don't stick up for themselves, which can attract users and bullies to them. This is harmful because it erodes their self-respect and they may consider doing themselves harm. Establish a zero-tolerance policy for people who behave in this manner in order to heal.

Twelfth house Martians were competitive, aggressive people in their past life and sometimes they retain the imprint of that experience by haunting the gym or otherwise being physically active this lifetime. This is absolutely necessary so they can let off steam.

Those with Mars in the twelfth house are often interested in debating the existence of aliens or paranormal experiences.

Don't be shy about telling people what inspires or motivates you. You may be surprised by how many like minds and opportunities will arrive if you share what turns you on.

★★★

JUPITER IN THE TWELFTH HOUSE

People with Jupiter in the twelfth house are usually compassionate, introverted, kind people who genuinely enjoy helping others. Don't be afraid to exhibit your warmth; people will still respect you even if they discover what a sweetheart you actually are. People with this placement would do very well working with those who are sick or in dire straits.

People with Jupiter in the twelfth house often feel they have an intimate connection with the creator and feel divinely protected as a result. Be mindful not to allow your legendary faith to descend into religious fanaticism or aggressive attempts to convert people to your point of view, and don't take insane risks involving dangerous or unstable people because you feel that you are being divinely protected. There is nothing unspiritual about being discerning.

If your religion or spiritual path involves the belief in guardian angels or tutelary deities, then it is suggested that you make communication with those forces a daily practice. Prayer and meditation brings this person clarity and peace of mind.

People with this placement should be mindful of biting off more than they can chew and of spending recklessly. Gluttony, over-indulgence, and extremism in general are easy for them to fall victim to and should be avoided; make sure those glasses of wine after work don't lead to an addiction. Balance is key.

In a previous life, you may have been a philosopher, a pillar of your religious community, or from an affluent family. As a result, you still have a desire to be an influential member of your community in this lifetime. Seek out groups that will welcome your desire to contribute in a positive and meaningful way.

✦✦✦

SATURN IN THE TWELFTH HOUSE

People with Saturn in the twelfth house avoid self-reflection, which is exactly what they need to get past the emotional blocks that prevent them from living their best lives. Unfortunately, there is a tendency for people with Saturn in the twelfth house to be overlooked by others even if they did all of the work. They won't speak up when this happens, but would prefer to brood instead.

Twelfth house Saturns may have been destitute or suffered soul-crushing losses in a past life. As a result, they may be afraid to relax and just enjoy their lives because there is a sense that tragedy could strike at any moment. This may manifest as a tendency to constantly complain or to allow the slightest inconvenience to ruin an otherwise good day or pleasant experience. Pessimistic and apathetic quotes claiming that things will never change are a clever ruse to avoid taking responsibility for one's life. Get out of your own way.

People with this placement often passed away before accomplishing a very important goal in their last lifetime. A sense of dread or an inexplicable feeling of dissatisfaction is often transferred to the current life. Just do your absolute best when you have a job to do and don't be so hard on yourself.

Twelfth house Saturns most likely knew their fathers in their previous lives. He might have been a strict disciplinarian, institutionalized or emotionally unavailable, or just really mean. This situation may have been duplicated this lifetime by being born to a dad that has the same or similar issues. The purpose of this is to find a pathway to healing in order to break this toxic cycle.

Those with Saturn in the twelfth house love solitude. Make sure you use that time alone wisely by reading inspirational books or meditating.

✦✦✦

URANUS IN THE TWELFTH HOUSE

People with Uranus in the twelfth house are people who are comfortable using their intuition to guide them. They seem to have knowledge from another time and are wise beyond their years. They may be a repressed or oppressed genius; people with this placement frequently get innovative ideas "out of the blue," and they may seem to contradict themselves a lot to people that are more linear thinkers.

Despite their intelligence and intuition, they are usually horrible at keeping secrets. They accidentally leak critical information without realizing what they have done. So even if they don't betray a confidence directly, they reveal so many clues that someone else can easily piece the puzzle together themselves. They are also often the recipients of leaked information.

They're the type of people who believe in many strange conspiracy theories and supernatural beings that others think are absolutely ridiculous or so highly improbable that they seem weird when they discuss these topics. The feeling that something is wrong with them, like they're essentially different from other people, can lead to fantasies about being part alien, demon, or angel. This feeling of "otherness" makes things like joining a secret society or other low-key organization that most people have never heard of attractive. They are tolerant of or may like the occult.

This is the least eccentric of the Uranus placements, so the twelfth house natives will most likely only behave unconventionally behind closed doors, though sometimes their weird quirks may make other people stop and stare in bewilderment. They may be prone to insomnia or strange sleeping patterns, or may prefer to sleep in an odd position or location. They may also be cheaters who don't feel bad about their illicit affairs.

People with this placement have a rebellious streak and may agree with the reasons to revolt but they are reluctant to admit it to others. They fear being locked up or being judged negatively by others that don't share similar views; they don't like being different because they fear an inevitable descent into madness or societal or communal exile if they color too far outside the lines. Healing and spiritual growth comes when they make a conscious effort to silence disempowering voices (internal and external) that try to frighten them into compliance. Stop being afraid to do your own thing and live this life as you choose!

✳✳✳

NEPTUNE IN THE TWELFTH HOUSE

People with Neptune in the twelfth house have the ability to become great mediums or psychics and should develop these skills.

These people often find daily, mundane life oppressive and find it difficult to cope. They are almost too deep to function without considerable effort. They need to be careful to avoid the tendency to rely on intoxicants as a form of escape.

Many people with this placement are attracted to communes, cults, and charismatic leaders whose motives may be very different than what they expect. Watch out.

People with Neptune in the twelfth house may experience visions or sensations from their past lives that they can't explain. They will feel a strong attraction to the aesthetic they were surrounded by last lifetime. They were most likely somehow detached from reality during their past life. Perhaps their ideas were ahead of their time, or they were always intoxicated, or they were mystics. As a result, twelfth house Neptunes may fantasize about living off the grid and leaving society completely behind. The physical plane in general is a drag to them.

Sharing your spiritual insights with others would work out nicely for you. You would give people a lot of things to consider and in turn would learn a great deal.

✳✳✳

PLUTO IN THE TWELFTH HOUSE

Those with Pluto in the twelfth house may find it therapeutic to donate or give away their old things as a way to psychically cleanse their space.

People with this placement often grow exponentially after experiencing a crisis or traumatic experience. This tends to surprise others who cannot imagine how they did it.

Sometimes people with Pluto in the twelfth house attract people who try to dominate, manipulate, or control them. When people like this are encountered, it's important not to make excuses for them or their behavior and to assert yourself.

Twelfth house Plutonians served humanity well during their past life and are now being called to focus on themselves in this lifetime. Unless death comes unexpectedly, they will reconcile the apparent dichotomy between good and evil on a personal level.

If you have Pluto in your twelfth house, you may feel torn between the need to be more reserved and the need to explore your passions. Instead of trusting your intuition, you may be missing precious opportunities due to indecisiveness. Try to find a way to pursue what makes you happy.

CONCLUSION

Putting It All Together

Three Water Triad Analysis Samples

✦✦✦

ANTOINE'S CHART

Fourth House Sign: Capricorn

Fourth House Planet: Jupiter

Eighth House Sign: Taurus

Eighth House Planet: Moon

Twelfth House Sign: Virgo

Twelfth House Planet: None

The key to Antoine's happiness is to seek a stable life that centers on close family, friends, and spirituality. Antoine loves predictability but the kind that doesn't automatically equate with monotony. For example, he's the type of person who would do well at a stable job that he likes doing, which pays him the expected amount regularly, but which may require him to move around or travel now and then. He would also feel renewed and refreshed by occasionally changing his perspective on things as soon as he sees his beliefs have become outworn or outdated. In terms of relationships, he feels most comfortable around

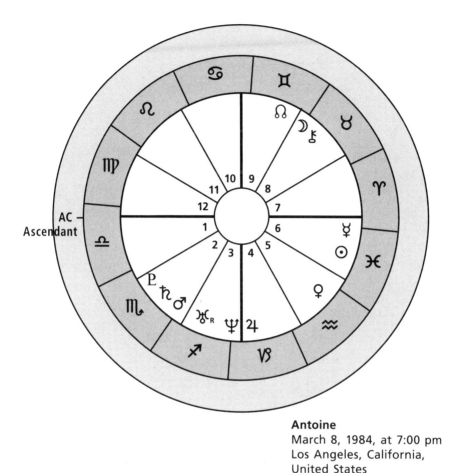

Antoine
March 8, 1984, at 7:00 pm
Los Angeles, California,
United States

people that he has a history with, and it's advisable for him to wait a while before letting new people into his circle of trust. He has a strong intuition, so he will automatically know when the time is right for that to happen. When it comes to romance specifically, Antoine would do best with a partner who is moral, highly principled, virtuous, faithful, and devoted to Antoine's well-being. This person can be introverted or extroverted, just as long as Antoine doesn't feel irrelevant, under-appreciated, or in danger of being cheated on. Everything and everyone in Antoine's world should be responsible and reliable.

✱✱✱

MORGAN'S CHART

Fourth House Sign: Pisces
Fourth House Planet: Jupiter
Eighth House Sign: Cancer
Eighth House Planet: Mars
Twelfth House Sign: Scorpio
Twelfth House Planet: Venus

The key to Morgan's happiness is to seek a quiet, tranquil life that is somewhat sedentary. If she is unwilling or unable to pack her stuff and move to a cabin in the mountains, then it is imperative that she maintains a strict stress-management program that involves purification. For example, she would benefit from regular visits to the sauna, seaweed wraps at the spa, salt lamps around the home, or joining a gym with a pool and swimming a few laps several times a week. Morgan is prone to extreme emotions, so maintaining a relaxation regimen will improve her physical and mental health exponentially as long as she sticks to it. In terms of relationships, she would be wise to keep her circle small. Morgan requires a lot of nurturing, and she needs it from people who she knows she can absolutely trust and who trust her. When it comes to romance, Morgan would do best with a partner who is more on the introverted end of the spectrum, extremely romantic, sexually uninhibited, and loyal. This person shouldn't be excessively flirtatious or in any way interested in arousing feelings of jealousy. Morgan's world should feel cozy and safe.

✳✳✳

DEVIN'S CHART

Fourth House Sign: Libra
Fourth House Planet: Sun
Eighth House Sign: Aquarius
Eighth House Planet: Neptune
Twelfth House Sign: Gemini
Twelfth House Planets: Saturn and Mercury

The key to Devin's happiness is to seek a life that is truly tailor-made for him. Any attempt to live according to a prix-fixe life plan that everyone else is following will engender a lifelong feeling of dissatisfaction. There are people in the world who have careers and lifestyles that expertly combine all the things that they are passionate about, and Devin would be wise to consider becoming one of them. For example, some people are paid to eat chocolate or are professional cosplayers! I'm sure they didn't imagine those things as viable career options when they were at job fairs in high school, but so what? Devin would benefit from reading about people who unapologetically live their lives according to their own rules. In terms of relationships, he would be wise to surround himself with eclectic risk takers who will offer him the encouragement he needs to pursue this handcrafted existence. When it comes to romance specifically, Devin would do best with partners more on the extroverted end of the spectrum, not clingy. Such people should be supportive of Devin's dreams and be way too busy in active pursuit of their own dreams to get in the way. Devin's world should be exciting and highly personalized to suit his tastes.

✳✳✳

It is my sincerest hope that my readers understand how much I care for them and want them to grow in their truth. A truth that can be shared with all but can only be felt by one . . . themselves.

Index

abuse, 33–34, 131–32, 150–51

acceptance, 48

Adam and Eve, 13

addictions, 32, 101, 108

Ahone, 11

Ailsie, 11

ambition, 59–60

ancestors, 14, 73, 125

anger, 33, 67, 113, 131, 138, 153

Aniyunwiya, 11

Antoine's chart, 160–61

anxiety, 129, 144

appreciation, 69

approval, 116

Aquarius, 27, 60–62, 85–87, 106–7

aquatic animals, 14

Aries, 23, 33–37, 66–68

arts, the, 32, 46

Astrodienst, 20

Atabey, 11

attention, 94–95

authentic self, 30, 33

balance, 118, 155

baths, spiritual, 9

beauty, 17–18, 101, 121

Benedict, Saint, 14

blame, 44, 85, 94, 100

Boriken, 11

boundaries, 1, 63, 96, 100, 108, 114, 140

bullying, 46, 105

burnout, 44

Caguana, 11

Cancer, 17–18, 24, 30–31, 42–45, 73–74, 95–96

Capricorn, 26, 58–60, 84–85, 105–6

celebration, 52

change, 32, 53, 77, 83, 86, 93, 144, 147

chaos, 72

charts, sample, 21, 160–64

cheating, 45, 157

cholera epidemic, 14

Christians and Christianity, 13–14

cleanliness, 49

cleansing, 9–10

Cochamama, 12